PRAYING GRACE
FOR
Women

55 Meditations
and Declarations
for Beloved
Daughters of God

DAVID A. HOLLAND

BroadStreet
PUBLISHING

BroadStreet Publishing® Group, LLC.
Savage, Minnesota, USA
Broadstreetpublishing.com

Praying Grace for Women: *55 Meditations and Declarations for Beloved Daughters of God*

Design and typesetting by Garborg Design Works | garborgdesign.com

Editorial services by Bab Coppedge | http://linkedin.com/in/babscoppedge

Printed in the United States of America.

21 22 23 24 25 26 8 7 6 5 4 3 2 1

Dedication

For Tracy, Caitlin, Grayson, Olivia, Cora,
Winnie, Ruby, Sadie, and Holland;

the women who grace my days.

Contents

Part III: Grace for Peace

Part IV: Grace for Breakthrough

Introduction

I know what you're thinking: *A devotional for women by a man?* My hope is that you'll give me the benefit of the doubt and dive into a few of the entries here before you dismiss me. I had compelling reasons to write the collection of meditations you hold in your hands.

For one thing, my journey through life has gifted me with a front-row seat for what daughters of God battle daily and what causes them to thrive in God. You see, I'm in my fourth decade of marriage to one such woman. I love and admire her more than I can express. I really, really like her, too. I know it's a cliché, but she is my best friend.

Together, we were gifted with three daughters who, by God's enabling grace, we've watched grow into remarkable women of God. Now our babies are having babies, and of our seven grandchildren, we count five girls in the mix. I've been surrounded by glorious femininity for about as long as I can remember.

I'm confident that if you were to ask any of these ladies if I have some helpful spiritual insights to share about appropriating God's abundant grace for rest, peace, intimacy with God, and breakthrough, I'd get a rousing endorsement from them. (At least from the ones who can talk.)

Secondly, spiritual truth is spiritual truth. I was profoundly encouraged to discover my previous book, *Praying Grace: 55 Meditations on the Finished Work of Christ*, had struck a chord with many women. I've heard from many who expressed profound gratitude for that devotional over the last few years and have let me know that they are on their fourth, fifth, or ninth pass through the work. I believe this collection will also find a treasured place on the nightstands and end tables of many women of God.

Allow me to share a couple of notes about the content. In several places here, I briefly quote preachers and teachers from the 1800s. Some, like Charles Spurgeon and Andrew Murray, are well known, while others are quite obscure. Yet all possessed some profound insights for us concerning God's grace and faithfulness. Because the writings I cite are well over 100 years old, they are in the public domain. So, in some cases, I have taken the liberty of modernizing the prose of the quote for clarity, while remaining faithful to the message and meaning of the author.

Finally, a word of explanation about the "Prayer of Declaration" you'll find at the end of each devotion. In Ephesians 6:18 (NIV), Paul exhorts us to "Pray…with all kinds of prayers and requests." Clearly, there must be numerous types of prayer, each one powerful and appropriate for its purpose. One such type is what I call "declaratory" prayer. These are prayers that put the truth of God's Word into your mouth in the form of a bold, faith-filled declaration. Your Bible is filled with them. There is something so powerful about this. I encourage you to say them out loud for two reasons.

First, when your own ears hear those words coming from your own mouth, something transformational happens in you. The second reason is this: Your ears aren't the only ones listening. Invisible angelic hierarchies hear you, too. If you had eyes to see spiritual dimensions, you'd see things moving and changing as you speak.

The meditations themselves are crafted to help you align your thinking ("renewing your mind" Romans 12:2) to the truth of *what* Jesus accomplished for you and *who* you truly are as a result. They are about transforming your sense of *identity*—rooting the truth of who you are in Christ deep into your heart.

This is not something that automatically happens when you become a daughter of God; it's a process. This book is designed to accelerate and facilitate that process. That means that the declarations may very well sound false in your ears when you first start proclaiming them. Even arrogant or boastful. If so, take that as an indicator that you *need* this process. Keep reading these meditations. Ponder the key scriptures and speak the declarations that are built upon them. Then watch what happens.

May the words on the pages that follow bring you hope, encouragement, strength, confidence, peace, and power.

David A Holland

I
GRACE FOR REST

Breathe

So we conclude that there is still a full and complete Sabbath-rest waiting for believers to experience.

HEBREWS 4:9

The relentless striving for perfection. The never-ending struggle to meet everyone's expectations. Heaven forbid you let anyone down or disappoint any of the multitude of people who are counting on you. Then there's your most brutal critic of all—your own inner voice. It's exhausting, isn't it?

What's worse, we often carry that same frantic dynamic right into our relationship with God. In fact, we often think of Him as if He's the fussiest, most demanding person in our lives. Too many daughters of God relate to Him as if He is a harsh, perfectionist father who simply can't be pleased. The dad you love and admire but who you're always disappointing. The one whose approval always seems just out of reach.

That is a false perception that the enemy of your soul is more than happy to help perpetuate. Here's the truth that destroys that lie. Hebrews chapter four describes salvation as an invitation to enter into an ongoing, never-ending "Sabbath rest."

The Sabbath was a designated day under the Old Covenant in which no one was to work or strive. It was created to be a blessing, but the Israelites ultimately turned it into another religious box to check, as we humans so often do. Another achievement to be proud of.

That's what religion does. It takes things God designed to bless and help us and drains them of all joy—turning them into yet another obligation to meet, rule to follow, or yardstick for measuring yourself against others.

Living life in this fallen, twisted world will always require effort. But God's invitation to "Sabbath rest" means that your relationship with Him shouldn't. In Jesus, the striving to please Him is over. Jesus pleased Him on your behalf. Daughter of God, you can lay down the struggle to qualify. Jesus was and is your complete qualification.

What's left is simply enjoying what Adam and Eve forfeited: enjoying God. Never again having to worry whether you've done enough to make Him happy. Never again fretting about measuring up to some impossible standard. Jesus measured up on your behalf.

Rest. Breathe.

GRACE DECLARATION:

Father, You have invited me to join You in an ongoing, never-ending Sabbath rest. I will not keep You waiting. Beginning today, I cease struggling to qualify for or earn Your love and acceptance. Jesus, You are my qualification. You measured up on my behalf. So, I rest in You. I breathe.

Discover the "Faith-Rest Life"

God's works have all been completed from the foundation of the world, for it says in the Scriptures, And on the seventh day God rested from all his works.... As we enter into God's faith-rest life we cease from our own works, just as God celebrates his finished works and rests in them.

HEBREWS 4:3B,4,10

The title of a 2017 article in *Psychology Today* magazine asked, "Why are Women so Exhausted?"[1] In it, the author, a clinical psychologist, pointed to the way women invariably end up being the default cultivators and keepers of relationships—family, friends, work, church, and community. If they don't do it, it often doesn't get done. Sadly, it's easy for your relationship with God to become just one more stressor in that juggling act.

This means that when many daughters of God think about turning to their heavenly Father, they get a knot in the stomach instead of the anticipation of refreshment, peace, and supernatural help. It need not be this way. Here's why.

For six days God was a flurry of creative activity. Day by day, order emerged out of chaos. Wonders of life, beauty, and complexity appeared. Each extraordinary phase of work was pronounced "good" at its completion. Then, after crafting and commissioning the crowning glory of His six-day masterpiece—mankind in two complementary forms, male and female—God rested.

That doesn't mean God entered a long period of total idleness, but only that His flurry of creative effort was finished. God's "sabbath" has been complete and ongoing. The fourth chapter of Hebrews makes it clear that God wants the same thing for you. And it is filled with both encouragements to "enter" that rest and earnest cautions about not having the faith to do so.

Faith? Yes, as that chapter makes clear, doubt is the primary enemy of your stepping into this faith-rest lifestyle. To our natural minds, God's offer of rest seems simply too good to be true. It can't possibly be that effortless, can it? It can. And it is. The "good news" of the gospel is that God really is ready and willing to accept Jesus' perfect life as a proxy for your flawed and broken one. If you've accepted His offer, God really has imputed Jesus' pristine righteousness to you and laid every last bit of your brokenness and sin on Him.

Yes, it's humbling. But accepting Jesus' finished work on your behalf means a complete and ongoing end to your efforts to create a pathway back to God. It means a full and forever end to trying to earn or merit your heavenly Father's acceptance and favor. You may have many difficult people in your life but your heavenly Father is not one of them. He's easy.

Oh, weary one, you have been invited into a lifestyle…the faith-rest lifestyle. God rested from His labors. Isn't it time that you rested from yours?

GRACE DECLARATION:

Father, although it seems too good to be true, I believe it. You want nothing from me except relationship. I can bring nothing to this transaction other than a childlike heart of belief in Your astonishing goodness and generosity. Today I rest *with* You. I rest *in* You.

Step Over

Now the promise of entering into God's rest is still for us today. So we must be extremely careful to ensure that we all embrace the fullness of that promise and not fail to experience it...So then we must be eager to experience this faith-rest life, so that no one falls short by following the same pattern of doubt and unbelief.

<small>HEBREWS 4:1,11</small>

You're standing in the desert wilderness. But over there, across the river, is the Promised Land. The wilderness has been a harsh, dry place filled with striving and struggle. You've needed miracles of provision just to survive.

But God has led you to this extraordinary place. It's a green, fertile place promising abundance and rest. It represents an end to both your wandering and wondering where your next drink of life-sustaining water will come. From the throne of heaven, God declared and decreed this land is yours. Now all you need do is believe what He said and act on that faith by "stepping over" into it.

Of course, we know how that first generation of Israelites responded to that choice. A fearful "bad report" by some of the spies sent out to explore the new land filled the entire nation with dread. As a result, they forfeited their opportunity to experience the "rest" that rightly belonged to them.

In the key scripture passage above, the author of Hebrews uses those Israelites' failure to enter Canaan as a metaphor for what many born-again believers do. They let fear and misbelief keep them in a wilderness of striving and struggling to "earn" what Jesus has already gifted them. And just as the spies planted fear in their hearts, many well-meaning teachers and preachers make them afraid they're not doing enough to earn God's blessings or making enough sacrifices to please Him.

Here's the truth, daughter of God. A loving Father drew you out of the slavery of sin and separation from Him. He's patiently led you through the harsh wilderness of pointless, fruitless, self-improvement, self-sufficiency, and self-consciousness. He guided you out of the shame and despair that result from repeatedly trying and failing to do all the things "good" Christians do.

With cords of kindness, He's drawn you to the border of a good land. A place of rest. A place where you know that you know you're accepted, received, and approved…in Jesus. The only remaining question is: "Will you cross over?"

Your Father, through the writer of Hebrews, pleads with you to uproot the fears and doubts sown in you by Religion. He says the only thing you need to "be careful" about is whether or not you've trusted Him enough to rest. Step over. The "faith-rest life" awaits.

GRACE DECLARATION:

Father, I will not make the same mistake that generation of Israelites made. I'm stepping over. I trust the "good report" that Jesus has met, on my behalf, every requirement for being a resident of this beautiful land. I choose the faith-rest life.

Humble Enough to Rest?

But he continues to pour out more and more grace upon us.
For it says, "God resists you when you are proud
but continually pours out grace when you are humble."

JAMES 4:6

We've seen that fear is a major obstacle to entering the Sabbath rest God has prepared for us through Jesus' finished work of love and grace. But it's not the only one. Rest has another enemy: pride.

Have you ever given someone an extravagant, unexpected gift simply because you loved them and wanted to bless them? Did that person suddenly feel obligated to do something for you in return? How did that make you feel? You weren't looking to conduct a transaction; you were trying to express your care and affection. You just wanted them to know they were valued.

Pride lies behind that uncomfortable reaction to generosity. Most of us simply have a hard time receiving. Yet a humble will-ingness to receive is literally the only requirement for entering God's rest. But it's a non-negotiable one.

This is one of the many differences between the Old Covenant system and the "new and better" covenant Jesus inaugurated through His death and resurrection. Under the old system, you didn't come to God empty handed. You brought an offering. A sacrifice. But under the new one, Jesus gave *Himself* as your offering. *He* was and is your sacrifice. That means we all come to the cross the same way: empty handed and in need. Recognizing that requires humility.

The passages in Hebrews we've been examining reveal that, at the spiritual level, "Sabbath rest" means leaning fully upon and into Jesus' finished work on the cross *with nothing added*. It means not insulting God's grace through pride-driven efforts to "pay back" or earn your place at God's table. It's a way of *being* that doesn't insult the staggering price God paid—namely, His only Son—to provide you with the extravagant gift of restoration (to Him) and rest (in Him) through trying to pay Him back.

So, you may be wondering... *What about good works? Didn't James say that faith without works is dead? Didn't Jesus tell us to let the world see our good works so they'll glorify God?*

They did, indeed. Here's the key to understanding these and similar exhortations. Simply keep in mind that your good works don't earn you your connection to God. That's a gift. But also know that good works *do* result naturally and organically from being in connection to God. In other words, your life-giving connection of rest as a beloved daughter of God can't help but produce good works in you.

God freely gives the grace of rest to the humble, because only the humble have open hands to receive.

GRACE DECLARATION:

Father, I come to You today the same way I came to You originally, with empty hands and a heart full of gratitude. I humbly receive what You have so abundantly provided. Today I lean fully, with all my weight, on Your goodness. And good works naturally flow out of my connection with You.

Lighten Up

Pour out all your worries and stress upon him and leave them there,
for he always tenderly cares for you.

1 PETER 5:7

Carefree! That's an evocative word, isn't it? What image comes to mind as you see it here in print?

There's a good chance you envisioned a child, most likely at play. Anyone who has lived for any amount of time in the adult world has—in a moment when the stresses, pressures, and complexities of life are weighing down—looked back longingly at simpler childhood days.

Of course, we all had worries as children. It's just that now, in the bright light of adulthood, we understand how trivial most of those worries were. Our grown-up concerns seem enormous in comparison.

The constant crush of financial pressure. The drain of navigating dysfunctional relationships with broken people. The gnawing feeling of inadequacy and inferiority that social media is so wickedly good at instilling and feeding. An inescapable electronic news and information ecosystem designed to fuel either fear or outrage in you because everyone on the internet gets paid through clicks, pageviews, and shares.

Carrying these weights in an environment of pandemics, protests, and political polarization is a prescription for the crushing of the human soul with care. Your soul.

Much of the substance abuse and addiction currently ravaging our society is driven by the desperate need to assuage the relentless pain of this pressure. Multitudes self-medicate to numb the ache; or seek escape through mindless, meaningless pursuits.

God did not design us to carry that weight. And here's wonderful news: His beloved children of all ages have access to a "carefree" life as their birthright. That is because the cross of Jesus Christ is an extraordinary place where a kind Father and gentle Shepherd partnered together to carry our griefs, sorrows, and weighty cares.

The great 19th-century preacher Charles Spurgeon (1832–1903) once said: "He took our griefs and carried our sorrows that we might be a happy people…Ours is the crown of lovingkindness and tender mercies, and we wear it when we cast all our care on Him who cares for us."

A life free of care (carefree!) is possible for you. Simply lay your burdens at the foot of the cross and pick up, in Spurgeon's words, your "crown of lovingkindness and tender mercies."

PRAYER OF DECLARATION:

Father, because You have poured Your love on me, You invite me to pour my cares out before You. Because You tenderly care for me, I can lay down my heavy bundles of worries, stresses, pressures, and fears. I am carefree. Because I am Yours, and You are mine.

Organic Fruit

"So you must remain in life-union with me, for I remain in life-union with you. For as a branch severed from the vine will not bear fruit, so your life will be fruitless unless you live your life intimately joined to mine. I am the sprouting vine and you're my branches. As you live in union with me as your source, fruitfulness will stream from within you—but when you live separated from me you are powerless."

JOHN 15:4—5

Picture a thriving, potted tomato bush, each branch laden with green and red ripening tomatoes. Now imagine taking some pruning shears and snipping off a branch of the shrub. Now visualize just leaving that amputated branch lying beside the pot. What happens in the days that follow?

Of course, the disconnected vine withers and dries up. And it certainly doesn't produce any additional tomatoes. Its days of fruitfulness are over.

Jesus had something very similar in mind when He told His disciples that He was, in a sense, a vine, and they were branches. He was revealing that when the New Covenant came, their spiritual connection to Him would be their source of life and power.

The same is true for you and every daughter (and son) of God. Apart from your life-union with Jesus, you cannot produce anything of eternal value.

"But what about good works?" you may ask. Good works are a natural outgrowth of being in connection to God through Jesus. They flow *organically* from being in life-giving connection to Him.

You don't qualify for becoming, or remaining, a child of God through any effort of your own. A gift is a gift. It can only be received. But once you become God's child, the most natural thing in the world is to begin exhibiting the characteristics of your Father. In other words, we don't do good works *for* our relationship with God; we do them *from* our relationship with Him. This is precisely what Jesus had in view when He shared this metaphor with His disciples.

Do you see it? You're not capable of bearing real, eternal fruit apart from your connection to Jesus. That means you don't have to strive, strain, or struggle to be fruitful when you're restfully connected to the Vine. As you "abide" in Him, that is, rest in His finished work on your behalf, you naturally can't help but bear fruit.

Plug into and rest in your blood-bought connection to Him. Then watch the fruit *organically* spring forth!

GRACE DECLARATION:

Jesus, I see it now. Striving in my own strength to *do* better, to *be* better for You, makes me like a broken-off tomato branch. Apart from You, I can do nothing of eternal value. But by simply resting, day by day, moment by moment, in life-union with you, I soon discover Your nature, Your desires, Your fruit, emerging organically from my life.

Choose Rest

"Are you weary, carrying a heavy burden? Come to me. I will refresh your life,
for I am your oasis. Simply join your life with mine. Learn my ways and you'll
discover that I'm gentle, humble, easy to please. You will find refreshment and
rest in me. For all that I require of you will be pleasant and easy to bear."

MATTHEW 11:28—30

Every mom knows this scenario all too well. The ordinarily
cheery toddler is angry, sad, exasperated, bored, and overstimu-
lated all at the same time. She's inconsolable and unmanageable.

Of course, the mother knows the real problem. She's over-tired.
Exhausted. Momma also knows that the only thing that will
put them both out of their misery is a nap. The child is spent and
needs rest. And yet, she refuses. She fights this obvious remedy
with all her pint-sized might.

A test of wills with a three-year-old is a terrible thing to behold.
And "will" is the key word here. Every human is born with a
will—the ability to choose, and refuse. That includes you.

The 19th-century Scottish preacher James Hamilton once
observed: "We are weary and heavy laden, and our heavenly
Father offers to carry us and our affairs in His own everlasting
arms. But we must consent to be carried to find rest for our souls."

One unchanging truth runs from Genesis to Revelation: God
respects our freedom to choose. God placed Adam and Eve in
the Garden with free will and the ability to choose. Every one

of their descendants inherited that same wonderful-terrible gift. The freedom to choose Him or reject Him. To run to Him or flee from Him.

Through Joshua, He challenged the Israelite tribes to "choose for yourselves today whom you will serve." (Joshua 24:15 NASB) Through Elijah, He asked, "How long are you going to struggle with the two choices? If the Lord is God, follow Him; but if Baal, follow him." (1 Kings 18:21 NASB) Jesus invited a wealthy young seeker of truth to leave all behind and follow Him on an adventure for the ages. The young man shrugged, passed, and walked away. Jesus didn't chase him.

Yes, Jesus invites and draws and woos us, but He never forces us to come. And as we come, He invites us to lay our burdens down, yet this, too, is our choice. It is one thing to know that He is willing and able to carry our greatest burdens, but something completely different to let Him.

In other words, we have to *choose* the rest He so freely offers. "Stop fighting me, little one," you hear Him saying. "It's time for a little rest."

GRACE DECLARATION:

Oh, gentle, humble Jesus, I choose the refreshment and rest You have graciously offered at the oasis of Your presence. I actively release my cares and burdens to Your strong hands as I cease my frantic striving to qualify for the favor You have already gifted to me. I choose rest. I choose You.

Stop Struggling and Nestle In

I am humbled and quieted in your presence.
Like a contented child who rests on its mother's lap,
I'm your resting child and my soul is content in you.

The original Hebrew in the above verse suggests a small child who has been weaned. In fact, many translations say, "like a weaned child upon his mother's breast."

Mothers who have nursed a child for at least a year will instantly grasp the imagery here. A one-year-old infant will frequently demand to be nursed—wriggling and squirming in a struggle to get into the nursing position while pulling at mom's shirt. Watching a mother try to carry on an adult conversation while wrangling a baby who has shifted into this mode is a bit like watching a jiu-jitsu match in which one fighter is much larger, but the other is relentlessly determined.

Such battles end once the child is weaned. From that time forward, mother's lap is purely a place of comfort, care, and connection. That is possible only because the maturing child has graduated from thinking of that intimate space as primarily "the place where my needs are met."

The psalmist David had this graduation in mind when describing his relationship with his heavenly Father. He recognized his (and our) tendency to make visits to God's presence solely and wholly a quest to find provision for what we think we urgently need.

In other words, for many believers prayer means one thing only: asking God for things. This type of prayer is, to use the old-fashioned church-y term, "supplication," and it represents only one of the many kinds of prayer mentioned in the Bible.

Please don't misunderstand. There is nothing wrong with bringing your needs, wants, dreams, and desires to God. In fact, the Bible encourages us to do so. In Philippians 4:6, Paul exhorts, "…with thanksgiving let your requests be made known to God." (NKJV)

However, there is a level of maturity and growth in God in which you frequently come to Him with no agenda other than to *be with* Him. Like David, you intentionally calm your soul and quiet the inner voices shouting with urgency. These encounters with God are not about our most pressing needs. Like the weaned child, they're more about *connection*. Presence. It is about being, in David's words, a "contented child,"—choosing to know that God Himself is enough.

You can only do this when your heart trusts in Him. When you're mindful that Jesus said the Father already knows what you need and is never reluctant to provide. (Matthew 6:8,32)

GRACE DECLARATION:

Father, today I quiet and calm my soul. I cease struggling and nestle in. I come to You not on a frantic quest to get things *from* You but to simply be *with* You. I trust You for the meeting of my every need. I am Your resting child on Your lap, and my heart is wholly and utterly content in You.

The Epic Poem Titled "You"

We have become his poetry, a re-created people that will fulfill the destiny
he has given each of us, for we are joined to Jesus, the Anointed One.
Even before we were born, God planned in advance our destiny
and the good works we would do to fulfill it!

EPHESIANS 2:10

Homer's *The Illiad* and *The Odyssey*. Dante's *The Divine Comedy*. John Milton's *Paradise Lost*.

These are widely considered to be among the greatest 'epic poems' of all time. But there is another powerful and moving epic poem currently being penned. This work-in-progress is the labor of love of the greatest storyteller the world has ever seen. The title of this unfinished work is…*your name*.

Most English translations of today's key verse say we are God's "workmanship"; another says "handiwork." The first brings to mind a well-constructed refrigerator; the second, some sort of craft project one of the kid's brought home from Vacation Bible School. The *New Living Translation* does much better by declaring, "For we are God's masterpiece…"

But it is *The Passion Translation*, reflected in today's key verse, that best captures the essence of what Paul wrote. The Greek word he used there was *poiema,* and you will instantly recognize its relationship to our English word poem. It means the creative work of an artist. Paul uses this word only one other time in his writings. In Romans 1:20, he says we can tell a lot about the Creator by looking at what He created (His *poiema*).

In Ephesians 2:10, Paul is revealing that at the moment you were born again, or "re-created," God penned the opening lines of a one-of-a-kind epic poem titled "You."

From the moment you were created, the Writer already had the broad outlines of the plot (your "destiny") in mind. "For I know the plans I have for you," says the Lord. "They are plans for good and not for disaster, to give you a future and a hope." (Jeremiah 29:11 NLT)

God is a master storyteller. A poet of unmatched talent and creativity. And this brilliant artist has set Himself to the task of crafting an epic narrative that displays His brilliance through *your* words, actions, and experiences. So, trust Him. Yield to Him, like soft clay in the hands of a master sculptor.

Yes, you are God's poetic work-in-progress. Many stanzas remain to be written. All of heaven eagerly awaits the lines that will be penned in the days ahead. What the heavenly hosts know for certain is that the outcome will be both good and lovely. For that is the unmistakable style of the Poet.

PRAYER OF DECLARATION:

Father, my life is Your poem to write. You began this story by joining me to Jesus. The plot features twists and turns, but the arc bends towards a hopeful future for me. I trust Your writing because I trust Your heart. I find comfort and peace in knowing that You are as good as You are brilliant. I yield myself to Your authorship. Display Your talent through my story.

A Vital Shift of Mindset

. . . If God has determined to stand with us, tell me, who then could ever stand against us? For God has proved his love by giving us his greatest treasure, the gift of his Son. And since God freely offered him up as the sacrifice for us all, he certainly won't withhold from us anything else he has to give.

ROMANS 8:31–32

Your connection to your heavenly Father is a relationship, not a transaction. It is based wholly upon the giving and receiving of a gift, not the earning of a wage or qualifying for a prize. This represents one of the most difficult mind-shifts to make in stepping into a lifestyle of grace, rest, and power. Yet, it is absolutely vital.

We've been programmed by our culture to think transactionally. It's deeply ingrained in us from childhood. This is why we have such a hard time comprehending the grace of God. Our interactions with God must always and only be relational. Doing more "for God" doesn't earn you more favor with Him. Nor does asking something big of Him require more deposits in some invisible account or more earned points on some heavenly tally sheet.

That's the very definition of "works"—trying to earn God's favor or blessing by performing the right actions enough times. It's a toxic, pride-driven, and insulting way to approach God that has been summed up in the saying, "Do good, get good. Do bad, get bad." That mindset has far more in common with the Hindu concept of *karma* than the good news of Jesus Christ.

God is not a vending machine into which we insert a necessary amount of payment—right living, righteous behavior, prayer, witnessing—in order to extract something in return. What a relief! Jesus is the One who, in a single transaction, paid the enormous price to put us in direct relationship with God. Now everything we need flows from that Father-child relationship.

Yes, we pray, and we do good to others, we share our faith, and we do other "good works." But we do all of these things as a natural outflow of the relationship we already have securely, completely, and irrevocably. Good works aren't a form of currency we use to pay for God's favor and help.

Yes, your fleshly pride wants to say, "God, I'm so grateful for all You've done for me. I'm going to spend the rest of my life paying You back!" Please don't. The only appropriate response to God's gracious, extravagant, generosity is…humble gratitude. God doesn't want what you can do for Him. He wants…you! God did not send "the gift of His Son" to restore you to good behavior. Jesus died to restore you to intimate relationship with your heavenly Father.

PRAYER OF DECLARATION:

Father, I love being in relationship with You. And Your unconditional love has freed me to let my light shine before others so that they can see my good works and glorify You. I will not insult Your grace by trying to "buy" Your favor or blessing. You have already lavishly given me the gift of Your Son. How will You not also, along with Jesus, graciously and freely give me all I need?

A Reassured Heart
in His Presence

We know that the truth lives within us because we demonstrate love in action, which will reassure our hearts in his presence. Whenever our hearts make us feel guilty and remind us of our failures, we know that God is much greater and more merciful than our conscience, and he knows everything there is to know about us. My delightfully loved friends, when our hearts don't condemn us, we have a bold freedom to speak face-to-face with God. And whatever we ask of him we receive, because we keep his commands.

1 JOHN 3:19—22

I call it "heart confidence." It's a major key to receiving from God in prayer. If your prayers seem ineffective and powerless it's rarely a result of reluctance to *give* on God's side. It's often a broken or stunted capacity to *receive* on our end.

Did you know that your ability to receive from God is directly tied to the level of confidence in your heart as you approach Him in prayer? It's true! The Bible calls this confident expectancy "faith," and it's a pretty important and powerful thing.

If you come to God with your heart condemning you, it is very difficult for you to reach out and take hold of, by faith, what God has already willingly provided. If you come to Him feeling unworthy, disqualified, and judged because of your mistakes and failings, your "receiver" is severely limited. But if you approach

God boldly and confidently because you know you're coming not on your own merits but in Jesus' merits and righteousness, your confidence and expectancy are high, and your receiver is big.

As the first verse above reveals, the goal is to have a reassured heart when in God's presence. The problem is that your own conscience can be pretty strict and harsh. But there is good news for you in the passage above: "God is much greater and more merciful than our conscience." He "knows everything" and loves us anyway.

However, you also must deal with another voice pointing out all your failings and mistakes. The Bible calls that voice "the accuser." (Revelation 12:10) Satan's goal is to keep you isolated and out of God's presence because He knows it is your connection to power and life. Silence him the same way Jesus did, with the Word of God. Personalize and quote Second Corinthians 5:21 to him: "For God made the only one who did not know sin [Jesus] to become sin for [me], so that [I] might become the righteousness of God through [my] union with him." (additions mine)

As you prepare to come to the Lord, quickly check the status of your heart assurance. Do you feel reluctance or hesitance about coming before God's throne of grace? If so, just take that as a signal to put yourself back into full remembrance that you are not coming in *your* righteousness. You have Jesus' righteousness. So, come with "a bold freedom to speak face-to-face with God."

Prayer of Declaration:

Father, You know me; You love me, and You are greater than my critical conscience. My heart is reassured and at rest in your presence. Because Jesus is my righteousness, my heart does not condemn me, nor does my enemy have grounds to accuse me. With a confident heart, I know I have all Jesus purchased for me with His blood.

Wondrous and Inexpressible Secrets

Who could ever wrap their minds around the riches of God, the depth of his wisdom, and the marvel of his perfect knowledge? Who could ever explain the wonder of his decisions or search out the mysterious way he carries out his plans?

ROMANS 11:33–34

They gave it the name "Yeti Crab." Back in 2005, researchers announced the discovery of a bizarre, never-before-catalogued kind of crab that looked like it was covered in long blonde fur. It was unlike any crab anyone had ever seen.

Each year marine biologists discover many new species of life no one knew existed. This shouldn't surprise us, given that oceans cover more than 70 percent of the earth's surface, yet roughly 80 percent of it has never been mapped or explored. The deepest part of the sea, the Mariana Trench in the western Pacific, is more than 36,000 feet deep. That means you could place Mount Everest at that depth and the peak would still be 7,000 feet beneath the water's surface.

In a similar way, you can live an entire lifetime in intimate fellowship with God and not come close to glimpsing all the aspects and dimensions of His glorious complexity and goodness. You can explore a new facet of the Father's loving character every day and never run out of new "species" of mercy.

The psalmist glimpsed the Father and exclaimed: "What mighty miracles and your power at work, just to name a few. Depths of purpose and layers of meaning saturate everything you do. Such amazing mysteries are found within every miracle that nearly everyone seems to miss. Those with no discernment can never really discover the deep and glorious secrets hidden in your ways." (Psalm 92:5–6)

The apostle Paul may have experienced more heavenly revelation than any person who ever lived. He was taught the secrets of the New Covenant directly by the risen Jesus. (Galatians 1:11–12) He was once caught up into heaven where he was told, "wondrous and inexpressible secrets *that were so sacred* that no mortal is permitted to repeat them." (2 Corinthians 12:3–4) Nevertheless, after contemplating the way God strategically crafted and executed His plan to redeem mankind, even Paul was compelled to write the words of today's key verse.

Richard Fuller (1804–1876) once observed, "God's truth and faithfulness are a great deep. They are like the ocean itself. Always there. Vast. Fathomless. Sublime. The same in its majesty and inexhaustible fullness, yesterday, today, and forever." What new wonder of His grace will you discover today?

PRAYER OF DECLARATION:

Infinite God, it's true. I'll never stop discovering new dimensions of Your mercy and goodness. Depths of purpose and layers of meaning really do saturate everything You do. Yet even in all of Your vast majesty, You still see me. You see *me*! Even better, You know me, and Your unchanging grace is ever reaching toward me.

Thousand-Generation Faithfulness

So now wrap your heart tightly around the hope that lives within us,
knowing that God always keeps his promises!

It's hiding back there in your history. You may not remember it, but it's there, lurking somewhere in the opening chapters of the story titled "You." That humiliating betrayal. That defilement of your innocence. That profound violation of trust at the hands of a parent, a teacher, a leader, or a friend—the sting of which prompted you to make a ferocious inner vow:

I will never totally trust anyone again. I will always be on guard. I will wrap my heart in barbed wire and stuff it with steel wool.

Who among us hasn't been let down, deeply disappointed, or (figuratively) stabbed in the back by someone close to us? Perhaps this is why so many believers struggle to trust God with their whole being. That inner child still residing in all of us seemingly can't shake the fear that our trust and innocence will be betrayed again.

Yet this is the same heavenly Father who moved heaven and earth to redeem you—drawing you with cords of love out of a kingdom of hellish darkness, bringing you into His domain of joyous light and love. (Colossians 1:13)

Here's wonderful news. The God who chose you, wooed you, adopted you, and made you His own can be counted upon. He will never ditch you, betray you, trick you, nor, above all, lie to you. Over and over, the Bible reminds us that God is utterly, infinitely *faithful*.

Several generations ago, Christian author and teacher C.J. Sodergren wrote, "God is indeed faithful. The word 'faithful' is repeated often in the Bible precisely so it won't escape the notice of those who are in need of a faithful God. Every page of the Bible, even where this word is not expressly mentioned, testifies of the faithfulness of God."

It's true. Your Father in heaven is utterly, perfectly dependable. He will never leave you nor forsake you. (Deuteronomy. 31:6 NIV) His love is rooted in the sacred power of covenant, and God keeps His covenant to a thousand generations! (Deuteronomy 7:9 NIV)

So, renounce that old inner vow right now. It stands as a barrier between you and countless good and pleasant things that await in communion with your Father. Relax. Trust. Without reservation, rest the full weight of your life and future on His goodness. You belong to a God who is infinitely trustworthy because He is infinitely faithful.

PRAYER OF DECLARATION:

Father, You are not a flawed human who can let me down or disappoint me. Your faithfulness is unfathomable. I rest in, rely upon, and rejoice in Your infinite faithfulness. I completely renounce any inner vows I've made in the past that would keep my heart from wholly trusting in You.

II. GRACE FOR INTIMACY WITH GOD

Mercy's Kiss

So now we draw near freely and boldly to where grace is enthroned,
to receive mercy's kiss and discover the grace we urgently need
to strengthen us in our time of weakness.

Hebrews 4:16

When, as little children, we're told about God, one of the first things we do is visualize Him on His throne in heaven. With the best of intentions, most of us are steered toward a mental picture of a stern and ancient giant sitting at an elevated judge's bench. But it's actually worse than that.

In an effort to motivate good behavior, we're encouraged to focus on the fact that the One sitting on that throne of judgment sees all and knows all, even our innermost thoughts. Of course, that is true. God *does* know us better than we know ourselves. And nothing is hidden from His sight.

But too often when we're young, that information is intended not to comfort but terrify us. Like the "Big Brother is Watching" posters in George Orwell's *1984*, we were supposed to see God as relentlessly scrutinizing every word, deed, thought, and impulse in a search for flaws in order to dole out punishments.

So, we learned to see God's seat of power as a throne of judgment for us. And naturally, we learned to approach it sheepishly if we approached it all. When there, if we dared raise our eyes from a posture of repentant shame, we fully expected to see disappointment in that Father-Judge's face.

All of this makes it deeply significant that Paul describes God's heavenly seat of divine power as a "throne of grace." And if grace characterizes God's nature and rule, and it does, why, then, do we often slink timidly into God's throne room with a sense of dread? Why do we expect an upraised hand rather than "mercy's kiss?"

Such dread is utterly inappropriate for anyone who has said "yes" to God's free gift of adoption and relationship. If you are in Christ, you are clothed in His righteousness, and Jesus' favor and acceptance before God have been fully imparted and imputed to you.

Boldly look into His face, child of God. Look into those eyes. You will find nothing but love and acceptance there. *But my mistakes?... My failings?...My innumerable flaws?* "What of these?" your heart may ask. Tell your heart this truth: You can come boldly to the Throne of Grace. There you will receive not only a joyous welcome but Mercy's kiss and heavenly help for your every need.

GRACE DECLARATION:

Father, I come to You today with bold joy and expectancy—enrobed in Your Son's flawless righteousness. The knowledge that You know my every thought and deed, and chose me anyway, comforts me. Because I'm beloved and accepted, I know I'll always find grace gifts of help and power and strength in Your welcoming arms; and nothing but love in Your eyes.

You Know That Voice

"...the sheep recognize the voice of the true Shepherd, for he calls his own by name and leads them out, for they belong to him. And when he has brought out all his sheep, he walks ahead of them and they will follow him, for they are familiar with his voice. But they will run away from strangers and never follow them because they know it's the voice of a stranger."

JOHN 10:3—5

No doubt you've seen one or more of the viral videos of small children, born deaf, at the precise moment a cochlear implant was activated. In such videos, we witness the moment these little ones hear the voice of their mothers for the very first time. It requires a heart of stone not to weep with joy along with all those in the room as these children light up in simultaneous delight and recognition.

The voice of your Jesus has much the same power to your born-again spirit. Of course, your experience of "hearing" His voice doesn't involve sound waves. Even so, when you "hear" it (inwardly), something inside your heart responds in delighted recognition.

The Holy Spirit—or "the Spirit of Jesus" as He is called in Acts 16:7 and Philippians 1:19—was specifically sent to be the Good Shepherd's voice in your life. Jesus said the Spirit's role was to comfort, help, lead you into all truth, and show you things to come. (John 16:12—15)

Nevertheless, many believers say they struggle to hear the voice of the Holy Spirit. But that claim runs counter to what Jesus plainly says in today's key passage. He said we would recognize His voice, and our instinct would be to follow it. He also added the comforting addendum that we would not be tricked into "following the voice of a stranger."

Later in the same chapter, Jesus bluntly says, "My own sheep will hear my voice and I know each one, and they will follow me." (John 10:27) Please notice that the Lord did *not* say, "My sheep. . . ought to follow Me." He didn't say, "My sheep should strive to hear My voice and, if they know what's good for them, they will do their best to follow Me."

No, Jesus' words are not a command to be obeyed; they are a statement of fact. In the verse above He simply made a three-part statement: (1) "My sheep hear My voice." (2) "I know them." (3) "They follow Me." That should settle our hearts and calm our anxious minds.

Woman of God, hearing and following Jesus isn't a burden to try to bear. It is a promise to receive. Receive it! He knows you. You hear Him. You follow Him. Be at peace!

PRAYER OF DECLARATION:

Oh, Good Shepherd, I thank You that my heart hears Your voice and responds to it. My inward ears are attuned to Your voice. I receive guidance, instruction, direction, correction, encouragement, and comfort from You easily and clearly. I receive Your promise that a stranger's voice I will not follow. Lead on today! I'm right behind You.

Your Father's Marvelous Love

Look with wonder at the depth of the Father's marvelous love that he has lavished on us! He has called us and made us his very own beloved children.

1 JOHN 3:1

In healthy homes, there is something very special about the bond between a daughter and her father. Ask any father of girls and he'll confirm it. I certainly can.

The research testifies of this as well. For example, numerous studies have shown that a girl is far more likely to begin smoking if her father smokes. In contrast, the smoking habits of a mother seem to have little statistical impact on girls. (However, a mother who smokes *is* more likely to produce sons who take up the addictive habit.)

For good or ill, the father carries an outsized influence on the formation of a girl into a woman.

The clear emerging picture is that well-fathered daughters simply tend to do better in life. Which makes the epidemic of fatherlessness in our culture a true crisis.

What kind of earthly father did you have? Did you grow up with a daddy who was present, kind, loving, and protective? If so, you were blessed indeed. Truthfully, fathers tend to be just as flawed and broken as the rest of us. As such, they usually fall far short of the ideal.

Whatever your situation might have been growing up, your experience does not have to be your only chance at a loving relationship as the child of a wonderful father.

In biological terms, you can't be born without a "father." The same is true when you are "born again." The Word of God makes clear that part of the miracle of the new birth is that God Himself becomes your heavenly Father—by supernatural "birth" and adoption. The "birth" part means you are literally born of God. And your "adoption" means He *chose* you!

Romans 8:15 declares, "For you have not received a spirit of slavery leading to fear again, but you have received a spirit of adoption as sons and daughters by which we cry out, 'Abba! Father!'" (NASB)

Deep, life-nourishing intimacy with God is your birthright. As today's key verse makes clear, He chose (or *called*) you. And having chosen you, He has lavished His marvelous Father-love upon you. You are a beloved, well-Fathered child.

Prayer of Declaration:

Papa God, I look with wonder upon the depth of Your marvelous love for me. I have received and perceive a "spirit of adoption" that propels me confidently into intimate relationship with You. You are present. You are kind. You are protective. And Your Father-love is transforming me from the inside out.

Come with Royal Boldness

This perfectly wise plan [to redeem and restore mankind and the world] was destined from eternal ages and fulfilled completely in our Lord Jesus Christ, so that now we have boldness through him, and free access as kings before the Father because of our complete confidence in Christ's faithfulness.

<small>Ephesians 3:11–12 [ADDITION MINE]</small>

Nearly everyone can recall from their early school years the dread that accompanied being called to the principal's office. As adults, being summoned unexpectedly to the boss's office often triggers similar waves of apprehension, anxiety, and even fear. Sadly, many believers adopt this same nervous mindset when they contemplate approaching their heavenly Father for help, guidance, or comfort. They tend to avoid the very One of whom Jesus said, "nothing is impossible." (Luke 1:37) What a tragedy this is.

The ruler who sits upon the throne of the universe is not a grumpy principal or a demanding, hard-to-please employer. The Faithful One who chose you and made you His own is neither a cruel tyrant nor an angry, vindictive monarch demanding to be appeased.

No, He is, above all, a Father—a good Father—and as such finds great joy in seeing and blessing His children. He longs to show them favor and delights in their well-being. What is more, through His brilliant plan—flawlessly executed in the birth, death, resurrection, and royal ascension of His Son, Jesus—you have become both a priest and a king. In the words of 1 Peter 2:9, you are a member of "a royal priesthood." (NASB)

In biblical terms, "priests" are those who can access God directly and engage Him directly on behalf of others. Of course, "royal" needs no explanation. And as today's key scripture explicitly states, we enjoy "free access as *kings.*"

Such audacious boldness in approaching God runs totally counter to the "religious" training most of us received. Many of us were taught to slink into His presence cowering with fear, and only after a good long session of self-examination, confessing, and repenting.

But please note: According to Ephesians 3, that bold confidence does not spring from *your* worthiness, *your* merit, or *your* qualifications. No, you have this free access to God's presence and power "because of our complete confidence in Christ's faithfulness."

Dear daughter of God, if you're chronically timid and shaky in your approach to your Father, take it as a sign that you need to increase your "confidence in Christ's faithfulness." A blood-washed believer like you need never hesitate to fly to your Father's arms of love.

PRAYER OF DECLARATION:

Holy Spirit, help me increase my confidence—not in myself, but in Jesus' faithfulness. Because of it, I am of the royal blood of Jesus Christ. I am bold. I use my "free access" as royalty to intercede on behalf of others, especially my loved ones. As a priest of the Most High, I can connect them to His goodness and power.

Know How to Make an Entrance

You can pass through his open gates with the password of praise. Come right into his presence with thanksgiving. Come bring your thank offering to him and affectionately bless his beautiful name! For Yahweh is always good and ready to receive you. He's so loving that it will amaze you—so kind that it will astound you! And he is famous for his faithfulness toward all.

PSALM 100:4—5A

"Draw near to God…," James 4:8 (NKJV) tells us, "…and He will draw near to you."

Any step toward God is ever and always met with Him taking many toward you. Recall the image of the father in Jesus' parable of the Prodigal Son. There we see a father scanning the far horizon for a growing speck that just might be the beloved child returning. On the day that speck appeared, the father broke into a full run to meet him. That's your heavenly Father.

You were created for intimate communion with Him. It's the very reason He sent His precious and only Son. Jesus died to make a way for you and every willing heart to return to the life-giving presence of the Father.

All of this means there's no "wrong" way to come to God. The important thing is just to come. But some ways of coming are indeed better than others. Today's key passage recommends coming into the Father's presence with "thanksgiving" and "praise." This is powerful advice.

When you begin to contemplate God's lovingkindness and graciousness toward you; when you spend a moment recalling the unmerited blessings, unearned rescues, and unrequested kindnesses; when you consider the magnitude of the gift that is Jesus…you put yourself in a posture of expectancy and joy. And such is the posture that best fits an approach to a Father who "is so loving it will amaze you—so kind it will astound you."

Don't come to God this way because it is the *only* way to come. It isn't. Don't come to God this way because it is the required way. It isn't. Come to God this way because it is wildly appropriate. Come with expectancy and joy because when you've accurately glimpsed the reality of God's goodness and the enormity of His grace, you can't come any other way.

Daughter of God, your Father is "always good and ready to receive you." Run joyfully now into Heaven's gates and right into His glorious throne room with a heart overflowing with gratitude and mouth spilling over with praise. Do this and you might overhear an angel saying, "Now there's a woman who knows how to make an entrance."

PRAYER OF DECLARATION:

Oh, Father, I come to You at this moment with a heart overflowing with gratitude and mouth filled with praise for Your amazing love, Your astounding kindness, Your abundant mercies, and Your redemptive brilliance. Thank You! Thank You! Thank You!

Wild, Confident Abandon

Jesus overheard them and said, "I want little children to come to me, so never interfere with them when they want to come, for heaven's kingdom realm is composed of beloved ones like these! Listen to this truth: No one will enter the kingdom realm of heaven unless he becomes like one of these!

Matthew 19:14

Our oldest daughter, now a mother of four, has crossed the milestone age of 30. But she still calls me "Daddy" and I love that. It takes me back to those days when our girls were small, utterly un-self-conscious, and therefore, hilarious—a source of endless delight and entertainment.

There was a brief season of time when she was around three in which I'd settled into a small, rented office in a modest little building. The offices were all arranged on either side of a long central hallway. Mine was located near the end of the hallway, toward the back of the building.

Those were lean, hard times for us financially. So, the best parts of the best days would be the times my wife would bring the girls up for a surprise visit to my drab, Spartan little workspace. I would hear the chime that indicated someone had opened the front door of the building, quickly followed by the rising sound of stumpy sneakered feet hitting carpet at a full gallop down the hallway. A few seconds later, my oldest would burst through my doorway with a giant smile, a giddy "Hi Daddy!" and body language that shouted, "I'm here! Isn't it wonderful!"

And it was. Oh, how it was. My sincere response was always one of delighted welcome. Outstretched arms. A hug. A gathering into the lap. A breathless request for the latest news from her world.

The one charging down that hallway was too young and unaware to have ever once considered that I might be on an important phone call, or in a bad mood, or upset at her for some act of disobedience I'd heard about earlier in the day. Those things never entered her mind. Nor should they have. No, she approached with wild, confident abandon—and usually with a request ready on her lips. "Can we go get pizza tonight? Mommy, said it's up to you."

There is a thoroughly biblical, immensely powerful secret to effective prayer hidden in those treasured little moments with my first-born. The best, most appropriate approach to your heavenly Father looks very much like my daughter's approach to me.

God spent thousands of years preparing to put a second-and-final "Adam" into the earth. Having done so, He allowed His sinless Son to have all of humanity's sin and shame laid upon Him as our substitute and sacrifice. He did all of this and more for one reason…to restore you and me to Him. To build a bridge back to His lap. Fly to Him daughter. I promise, He will be delighted to see you.

Prayer of Declaration:

Father, You are not grumpy. I'm not an interruption. You're not too busy. You've been hoping I'd visit. I have things to tell You. But I know You have things to tell me, too. Wisdom and guidance to share. Gifts to impart. But above all, You moved heaven and earth simply so we could enjoy each other again. So here I come!

A Tenacious, Relentless, Stubborn Love

God, everyone sees your goodness,
for your tender love is blended into everything you do.

PSALM 145:9

Watching a sunrise from a mountaintop. Viewing a meteor shower on a clear, moonless night far from the lights of the city. Catching a glimpse of a hummingbird darting and hovering between blooms in a garden. The sudden breach of a humpback whale. The sight of glistening drops of morning dew on the strands of an intricate spider's web.

It was with moments such as these in mind that Thomas à Kempis (1380–1471) wrote: "There is no creature so small and insignificant, that it doesn't display the goodness of God." Most of us have experienced a sense of holy awe and an almost mystical sense of spiritual revelation when beholding something wonderful in the natural world. In those moments, we correctly sense God is both brilliant and kind.

This shouldn't surprise us. As Paul pointed out to the believers in Rome, profound truths about God and His character—His "invisible attributes"—are embedded in creation itself. (Romans 1:20) Even in Earth's current fallen, twisted state, nature cannot help but testify that God is good.

The truth is, you have placed your life in the hands of a Father who is so attentive and caring that He takes note of the struggles of sparrows. The same Artist who takes the time to paint hillside canvases with wildflowers and western skies in stunning pastel tones sees you. Knows you. Loves you. And that love is of a very special type.

It is a love embodied in the Hebrew word *hesed*—a word that appears 250 times in the Hebrew Old Testament. Some translations render *hesed* as "lovingkindness" or "steadfast love." In other places its rendered "mercy," "loyalty," or "devotion." It is a word that speaks simultaneously of God's unwavering faithfulness and tender care. It is a rich, multifaceted word that speaks of God's "covenant love" for you.

Because it is *love*, it is kind, merciful, and compassionate. Because it is *covenantal*, it is tenacious, resilient, and irrevocable. It's relentless and stubborn. This is unconditional love. A love for which you can't disqualify yourself no matter how wayward and ornery you get.

Your heavenly Father's faithful *hesed* love and care are on display in your own life if you'll only have eyes to see it. It's blended into everything He does for you and says to you. Ask the Spirit to open your eyes right now. Then look back across the expanse of your life and note the ways He's been good to you.

Prayer of Declaration:

Father God, please give me a deeper, fuller revelation of Your goodness. Help me see Your magnificent, redemptive, relentless *hesed* love on display all around me and in my own life. Knowing how resilient Your love is fills me with gratitude and comfort. Your tenacious, stubborn love has attached itself to me. So, I'm safe and secure in Your care.

Restored Treasure

I pray with great faith for you, because I'm fully convinced that the One who began this gracious work in you will faithfully continue the process of maturing you until the unveiling of our Lord Jesus Christ!

PHILIPPIANS 1:6

It's called "mudlarking." In London, *mudlarks* are people who walk the muddy banks of the River Thames at low tide in search of lost treasures. They find them with astonishing frequency.

It's not unusual for a searcher to dig up a 2000-year-old roman coin, a Viking sword, Saxon jewelry, or other lost treasures from the past. You'll find many of these historic finds on display today at the British Museum in London.

When a mud-caked artifact is extracted from the smelly muck of the Thames after centuries of burial, it's not a pretty sight. But often, after careful cleansing and restoration, something extraordinary, and frequently even priceless, emerges.

So it was with you and me. A tenacious Redeemer came mud-larking through the mire of this fallen, broken earth. He found us buried in sin, and with gentle care, extracted us from our prison of defilement. He carried us to His domain and washed us thoroughly. Then He lovingly began a painstaking process of restoration and beautification. It is He who began this "good work" in us. And it is He who can be counted on to faithfully see it to completion.

Thomas De Witt Talmage (1832–1902) once observed, "The chief beauty of grace is found in the soul. That grace takes that which was hard, and cold, and repulsive, and remakes it new and lovely. It pours upon your nature what David calls 'the beauty of holiness.'"

Nothing we can bring to our Father is so corrupted or spoiled that it cannot be made new by His love. There is nothing that the fragrance of His grace cannot make lovely. There is no darkness in our souls that cannot be scattered by the light of His love and mercy.

Jesus, the "Mudlarker from heaven," comes alongside us saying, "Behold, I am making all things new." (Revelation 21:5 NASB) The Artisan of the Universe proclaims, "All that is related to the old order has vanished. Behold, everything is fresh and new." (2 Corinthians 5:17)

What buried treasure He found when He came across you! Cleansed and lovingly restored, you now display His love and kindness to a watching world.

PRAYER OF DECLARATION:

Heavenly Father, You rescued me. But You did more than that; You transformed me, and You continue to do so. Thank You for choosing me just as I was. And thank You for committing to the process of restoring me—moment-by-moment, day-by-day—from the inside out, through the power of Your love and grace. You're pouring into me, "the beauty of holiness."

Necessary Extravagance

When the extraordinary compassion of God our Savior and his overpowering love suddenly appeared in person, as the brightness of a dawning day, he came to save us. Not because of any virtuous deed that we have done but only because of his extravagant mercy.

TITUS

Bring up the subject of the most extravagant weddings in modern memory and the 1981 ceremony of Prince Charles and Diana Spencer is sure to pop up. Diana's horse-drawn carriage, sapphire ring, and stunning dress were the stuff of fairy tales, and fueled the dream-wedding visions of an entire generation of girls.

Younger participants in such a conversation would likely mention the 2014 wedding of Kanye West and Kim Kardashian—two of the biggest celebrities in the world at the time. The (now-divorced) super-couple's wedding celebration spanned two European cities (Paris and Florence) and featured John Legend and Andrea Bocelli as entertainment. The Italian half of the festivities alone was estimated to cost $2.8 million.

But neither of these events can hold a candle to the most recent monument to nuptial excess and unnecessary extravagance. At or near the top of the list of the most opulent weddings *ever* sits the 2016 exchange of vows of Said Gutseriev, the son of a Russian billionaire oil mogul, to Khadija Uzhakhovs, a dentistry student at Moscow University.

An article in the British edition of *Elle* magazine describing this event carried the headline, "Welcome to the Most Insane Wedding Ever." At the center of the event, rumored to have cost the father of the groom roughly $1 billion (yes, that's *billion* with a "b"), was a bride dripping in several pounds of diamonds and wearing a dress so heavy with beadwork, the bride required assistance ascending stairs. Reception entertainment came courtesy of Jennifer Lopez, Sting, Enrique Iglesias, and other notables.

Even so, this spectacular event cannot hope to compare to the lavishness God displayed in wooing a bride for His only begotten Son. The price He paid was…that Son. Today's key verse correctly points us to the "extraordinary compassion" and "overpowering love" that God displayed in sending Jesus to earth, not to just die *for* us but to die *as* us. All of this was done not because we were deserving but rather was driven wholly by His "extravagant mercy."

The psalmist David had our Father's opulent generosity in mind when he wrote, "O God, how extravagant is your cherishing love! All mankind can find a hiding place under the shadow of your wings." (Psalm 36:7) What a price He paid to make us His own. What extravagance! What lovely, necessary extravagance.

PRAYER OF DECLARATION:

Father, You lavished Your love and mercy upon me. You are indeed extravagant beyond description. It is a love I did not deserve, yet You poured it out upon me anyway. You are generous. You are kind. And I happily find a hiding place under the shadow of Your wings.

Debt Free

When he had sipped the sour wine, he said, "It is finished, my bride!"
Then he bowed his head and surrendered his spirit to God.

JOHN 19:30

Have you ever borrowed money from a friend and then found yourself unable to pay it back? Or perhaps you were on the other end of that proposition. Maybe a friend in a desperate situation borrowed a significant sum from you and couldn't repay it in a timely way. You were likely glad to do it. Perhaps you were in no hurry to have it paid back.

Nevertheless, you know what happened. The borrower started avoiding the lender as if she had the Ebola virus. It's a sad but very common phenomenon. Even among the closest of friends, *embarrassment and shame keep debtor and lender apart as long as the obligation exists.*

This same dynamic was in place for thousands of years in mankind's relationship to God. Adam and Eve's sin put them (and us) in deep debt to God's eternal, immutable bank of justice. And as with the kind friend who lent us money, they instantly began avoiding Him.

This truth explains something mysterious Jesus shouted from the cross in the final moments of His life. Witnesses gathered around the dying Savior were puzzled to hear Jesus yell a Greek accounting term: "Tetelestai!" Our English Bibles usually translate that term with something along the lines of, "It is finished!"

But those three words are far too weak and one-dimensional to do *tetelestai* justice. The Greek speakers of Jesus' day knew that to declare a thing *tetelestai* is to rule that: "All has been accomplished. Everything formerly lacking has now been supplied. The wound has been healed. The obligation met. The debt satisfied completely."

Jesus' *tetelestai*! declared an end to our religious striving to repay our immense debt. God Himself had come down and done what no fallen human could do. That is, satisfy our staggering spiritual obligation to justice.

Powerful, grace-based praying begins with an understanding of Jesus' cry of *tetelestai*. "Praying grace" starts with the humbling, liberating realization that all the work of restoration has been done. All that remains is to receive it.

Your heavenly Father sent Jesus to pay your debt in full. Through His sacrifice, the demands of holy justice woven into the fabric of the universe at the moment of creation have been fully satisfied. You can now rejoice in the glorious truth that you can come to Him with no sense of obligation, indebtedness, or shame.

PRAYER OF DECLARATION:

Lord Jesus, I will not insult Your grace by seeking to add a single thing to a work You declared complete with Your shout of "*tetelestai*." Nor will I try to pay against a debt You have previously declared "paid in full." I will humble myself and gratefully receive everything You died to provide for me; everything Your Word declares is mine.

Back to the Garden

Yahweh is my best friend and my shepherd.
I always have more than enough.
He offers a resting place for me in his luxurious love.
His tracks take me to an oasis of peace near the quiet brook of bliss.
That's where he restores and revives my life.

We are stardust, we are golden,
and we've got to get ourselves back to the Garden.

You have to be of a certain age to recognize those words as the chorus of "Woodstock," a 1970 Joni Mitchell song describing the epic music festival that captured the imagination of the world in 1969. People spoke (and sang) of the Woodstock festival in reverential, sacred terms for good reason. It served as a giant religious gathering in hedonistic celebration of the ideals of the "peace and love" hippie movement.

That movement was "utopian" in that it sought, through human effort, to restore mankind to the idyllic place where, deep down inside, we all know we belong. The rebellion of the first human couple required—for their own good—their ejection from paradise. Since then, the heart of every human ever born has carried a longing…an ache…to be restored to what we were created for. Namely intimate, unashamed fellowship with our Creator-Father.

Adam and Eve's labor to create fig leaf garments to cover their shame represents mankind's very first religious work. Cain's rejected offering was the second. And so it has gone throughout history. From the Tower of Babel to the meticulous rules and regulations of the Pharisees, from every other world religion that invariably calls for sacrifice and self-denial right up to our modern idolatries—fallen man's impulse has been to work or earn our own way back. Joni Mitchell was spot on in character-izing this as a quest to "*get ourselves* back to the Garden." But that is utterly impossible.

The coming of the Son of God to Earth revealed that the Father had a very different plan for restoring us to His fellowship and blessings. One which would require nothing from us except the humility to recognize that we had nothing to contribute to our redemption. That our religious strivings were disgusting, smelly rags. That all we could do was humbly receive and be led by the Shepherd back into the green pastures and still waters of the Garden.

The Garden is not heaven by-and-by. It's now. In Christ, we have been restored to what Adam and Eve lost: intimate fellowship with God, the ability to stand before him naked and unashamed and to eat freely from the Tree of Life.

We could not get ourselves back to the Garden. But Jesus could. And did.

Prayer of Declaration:

Father, I recognize and accept that I have nothing to contribute to my redemption. Forgive me for ever trying to "sew fig leaves" to cover my sense of shame or build my own tower of good works back to communion with You. Oh, Good Shepherd, You have led me back into the Garden of the Creator's presence and to the sweetness of fellowship with Him.

The One Who Delights to Bless

Those who are loved by God, let his love continually pour from you to one another, because God is love. Everyone who loves is fathered by God and experiences an intimate knowledge of him. The one who doesn't love has yet to know God, for God is love.

1 JOHN 4:7—8

I was six years old and had just memorized my first Bible verse in Sunday School. Afterward, I proudly recited it for my parents. I discovered later that it was only a fragment of today's key verse, 1 John 4:8, that I had learned: "God is love." But it was a wonderful way to begin my understanding of God's nature and character. I've written a million-plus words about Him over the ensuing 55 years, yet I'm not sure I can improve on that three-word sermon, even today.

God *is* love. It's what defines Him, describes Him, moves Him. Yet there are many strains of Christianity that seem to delight in portraying God as a fierce, wrathful Judge-King searching for tiny reasons to disqualify His subjects from receiving any of His blessings while simultaneously watching for opportunities to dole out punishments.

Here is wonderful news: The ruler who sits upon the throne of the universe is neither a cruel tyrant nor an angry, vindictive monarch demanding to be appeased. He is, above all, a Father—a good Father—and as such finds great joy in blessing

His children. He longs to show us favor and delights in our well-being.

When blood-washed believers approach that glorious throne and look into the face of the mighty One who sits upon it, they find nothing but perfect love there. No anger, no annoyance, no disappointment.

Andrew Murray, the amazing missionary to South Africa and deep man of prayer, once wrote: "Look up and see our great God upon His throne. He is Love—and filled with an unceasing and inexpressible desire to communicate His goodness and blessedness to all His creatures. He longs and delights to bless."

It's true. God's wrath against sin has been utterly spent. It was poured out upon His own Son at the cross.

God is love personified and He delights in blessing you. May His Spirit open the eyes and ears of your spirit and reveal the height, depth, and breadth of God's love for you. When He does, you'll enter His throne room joyfully and with a heart filled with gratitude.

Prayer of Declaration:

I declare today that when I look into Your face, I see love in Your eyes, acceptance in Your face, and kindness in Your voice. I worship You. And I make my requests known to You in confidence. You are good. Your unfailing love continues forever. And Your faithfulness continues from generation to generation. You don't just *have* love. You *are* love.

"Welcome In!"

And since we now have a magnificent High Priest to welcome us into God's house, we come closer to God and approach him with an open heart, fully convinced that nothing will keep us at a distance from him. For our hearts have been sprinkled with blood to remove impurity, and we have been freed from an accusing conscience. Now we are clean, unstained, and presentable to God inside and out!

<small>HEBREWS 10:21–22</small>

I pastor and oversee "house churches"—fellowships that meet in homes. This certainly isn't the only way to do church, but it's a lovely one. Among the advantages is the intimacy and community that's easily established in that informal setting. But that very same intimacy also creates one of the biggest drawbacks to this model of community. It is not quite "visitor friendly."

New people are *far* less likely to show up at someone's residential doorstep than to an open-to-the-public building on the corner with service times proclaimed on a marquee. A person's house is a special, private place. You only arrive once you've been invited. And you only enter once one of the head of house has clearly welcomed you in.

God has a house. It's not a church building; it's an invisible, global home for all of His people. It contains many "dwelling places." (John 14:2) If you're born again, it means that at some point, the Holy Spirit issued an invitation to you, and you accepted.

And as today's key passage reminds us, when you showed up on the doorstep, the head of God's house, its "High Priest," Jesus, warmly welcomed you inside.

But as this verse also makes clear, once inside, it's still possible to shyly and reticently keep your distance from the Father who is waiting to feast with you at the banquet table in the heart of the home. You can linger awkwardly in the foyer and other perimeter rooms and miss the richest blessings of having been invited in. Many Christians do. How tragically unnecessary this is!

Why do believers do this? Today's key passage suggests that it is an unwarranted, inappropriate sense of unworthiness or uncleanness that keeps us "at a distance." These verses point us to the truth if only we'll have eyes to see it and the child-like faith to believe it.

You heart has been "sprinkled clean with blood to remove impurity." You have been "freed from an accusing conscience." You are "clean, unstained, and presentable to God inside and out!" All of this means you can approach Him with "an open heart."

Don't stand in the foyer. God sent His messenger Holy Spirit to expressly invite you to come. The High Priest of the House of God has warmly welcomed you in. Come closer. You belong here. There is an empty chair at the table waiting just for you.

Prayer of Declaration:

Sweet Father, forgive me for ever lingering at a distance when You have cleansed and purified and qualified me completely to enjoy life at Your banquet table. I choose to believe what Your Word says about me. The precious blood of your Son has cleansed my heart and my conscience. I am unstained. Wholly and fully presentable to You. I draw near to You right now.

With Him is Where You Belong

The parents kept bringing their little children to Jesus so that he would lay his hands on them and bless them. But the disciples kept rebuking and scolding the people for doing it. When Jesus saw what was happening, he became indignant with his disciples and said to them, "Let all the little children come to me and never hinder them! Don't you know that God's kingdom exists for such as these?

MARK 10:13—14

At our house, we called it "the welcome." When our three daughters were small, my arrival at the back door at the end of my day was greeted with a raucous celebration. Delighted squeals of "Daddy's home. Daddy's home!" filled the air, accompanied by the approaching sound of a stampede of little feet.

This blessed highlight of my day was a gift from my wise wife, who never did me the disservice of using my impending arrival as a threat: *"Wait until your father gets home!"* On the contrary, throughout the day she pointed to my eventual arrival as a promise to be eagerly anticipated, not a thing to be dreaded.

If we have ears to hear, the Holy Spirit of God is always doing something similar. He urges us to run to Jesus. He whispers that we are beloved and welcome. That His presence is the place we most *belong.*

Back in the Garden, after the fall of mankind, the very first sign that something terrible had been unleashed upon the world and within the hearts of God's beloved people was their impulse to hide when they heard the approach of His footsteps. We should take note that when sin and shame entered the very first hearts, God did not hide from them. On the contrary, He came looking for them!

Jesus says, "Behold, I'm standing at the door, knocking. If your heart is open to hear my voice and you open the door within, I will come in to you and feast with you, and you will feast with me." (Revelation 3:20) Why, then, are we so often reluctant to open that door? Why would we ever feel dread or shame at the sound of that knock? Or decline the opportunity to feast with Him because we feel unworthy?

Such responses are utterly inappropriate for any woman who has said "yes" to God's free gift of adoption and relationship through Jesus. These all insult the Spirit of Grace.

If you are a daughter of God, your approach to Jesus can and should be the joyous, unselfconscious run-and-leap of a small child into the loving arms of a beloved father. And when He arrives at your threshold, the most natural thing to do is throw open the door.

PRAYER OF DECLARATION:

Jesus, with You is where I belong. You welcome me with open arms, and I do the same with You. I feast in Your presence—dining sumptuously on Your extravagant love, abundant grace, infinite wisdom, and boundless strength. My door is always open to You.

III. GRACE FOR PEACE

Letting Go of the Stick of Fear

Love never brings fear, for fear is always related to punishment. But love's perfection drives the fear of punishment far from our hearts. Whoever walks constantly afraid of punishment has not reached love's perfection.

I JOHN 4:18

Parents instinctively use fear as a training tool for very small children. And rightly so. Curious, clueless little ones must be taught to avoid fascinating open flames, beckoning electrical outlets, overly friendly strangers, and the large fascinating dog on the other side of the busy street.

As children get older, most parents continue to utilize the tool of fear to encourage good choices, but only because we want the best for our kids. We love them and want them to live great lives and become happy, productive adults. We use fear as a training tool. As today's key verse explains, "...*fear is always related to punishment.*" We could substitute the words "negative consequences" and that truth would still hold.

Parents raising children have something in common with pastors. Both are responsible for training a group of people. Just as parents love their children, pastors love their flocks. They too want to see those under their care making good choices, doing all the "oughts," and avoiding all the "ought nots."

That noble goal leads many to present God as harsh, hard to please, quick to punish—a stickler prone to disqualify for small technical violations. They keep the sword of negative consequences dangling over the heads of their congregations.

Frankly, this is precisely why many well-meaning pastors resist the full implications of New Covenant grace. Despite all the New Testament reveals about rest and ceasing from our works, many continue to present a fear-sprinkled gospel of, "Do good. Get good. Do bad. Get bad." They are nervous about letting go of the stick of "fear" they believe keeps people doing "the right thing." *They are literally afraid to let us stop being afraid.*

Roughly 150 years ago, the Scottish preacher Alexander MacLaren read today's key verse and grasped how a fear-soaked approach was incompatible with a revelation of God's love. Thus, he wrote: "The love that casts out all fear does so because we have no part to play in it except to open our eyes and see that God has no anger—but rather is perfect, and absolute, and infinite Love."

Once you get a supernatural revelation of God's love for you—its astonishing depth and incomprehensible height—the fear of punishment will be driven far from you. And you'll do the things that please Him because you love Him, too.

PRAYER OF DECLARATION:

Father, Your extraordinary grace and unfathomable love are transforming me into the person I always wanted to be but could never become cowering under the "stick of fear." It is Your kindness that leads me to repentance. Your perfect love has driven out my fear. I want to please You because I love You.

The Universe is Sending You a Message

. . . from the creation of the world,
the invisible qualities of God's nature have been made visible,
such as his eternal power and transcendence.
He has made his wonderful attributes easily perceived,
for seeing the visible makes us understand the invisible.

ROMANS 8:20

You've felt it. It might have been on a clear summer night far away from the lights of the city as you stood transfixed by a sky impossibly full of shimmering stars. It might have been while standing on a high coastal bluff overlooking crashing ocean waves as a sinking sun painted the sky in blended pastels. Perhaps it was on a crisp autumn day when the trees seemed nearly luminescent in vivid hues of fuchsia, gold, crimson, and yellow.

Wherever it was, at that moment, you not only knew God was real, but that He was extraordinary.

Paul told the believers in Rome that many profound truths about God and His character—His "invisible qualities"—are embedded in creation itself. Even in Earth's current fallen, twisted state, nature cannot help but testify that God is mighty, brilliant, and good. On various occasions, Jesus pointed to birds, fish, sheep, flowers, and trees as illustrations of God's tender care and provision for His children. The psalmist said it this way:

> God's splendor is a tale that is told, written in the stars. Space itself speaks his story through the marvels of the heavens. His truth is on tour in the starry vault of the sky, showing his skill in creation's craftsmanship. (Psalm 19:1)

You have entrusted your life and future to a Father so attentive and kind that He makes the well-being of birds and flowers His concern. You are far more significant in His eyes than these. He sees your struggles. He knows your thoughts. He loves you.

The Old Testament frequently speaks of God's "loving-kindness." The Hebrew word behind that English term is *hesed*—one that speaks simultaneously of God's faithfulness and tender care. It is the word for God's "covenant love" for you.

Your heavenly Father's faithful love and care are fully on display in your own life if only you'll find eyes to see. Look around and note the ways He's been good to you.

Yes, the universe is speaking to you. At times it shouts. In other moments it speaks in a subtle whisper. Yet the message is always the same: "The God who chose you to be His own is glorious beyond description, powerful beyond comprehension, and utterly, unfailingly...good."

Prayer of Declaration:

Father, I open the eyes of my heart to see Your majesty all around me. By Your Holy Spirit, I'm receiving a deeper, fuller revelation of Your goodness. I see Your magnificent, redemptive love on display all around me and in my own life. Oh, how great is Your loving-kindness toward me.

A Mystery Revealed

*Jesus replied, "Philip, I've been with you all this time
and you still don't know who I am?
How could you ask me to show you the Father,
for anyone who has looked at me has seen the Father."*

JOHN 14:9

It is Thursday morning, September 8, 1504, in Florence Italy. In the center of the city's *Piazza della Signoria*, stands a mystery. Overnight, in the heart of the cobblestone plaza, a 17-foot tall "something" has appeared and is shrouded in a massive sheet of linen cloth.

Among the people of Florence, there is widespread speculation and debate about what that sheet hides. The way the sheet hangs offers only a few hints about this new *thing's* nature and purpose.

Later that day, city officials gather to reveal the mystery to the intrigued public. The unveiling introduces the world to something the famous artist Michelangelo has been secretly laboring over for more than two years. A hard tug on the cover reveals... his iconic sculpture of *David*.

For thousands of years, the true nature of God was similarly shrouded in mystery. Sure, there were a few tiny hints and glimpses of Him in the ancient Scriptures. But *who* God was and *what* He was like remained largely unknown.

We no longer have to wonder about God's nature, character, or disposition. Jesus was God revealed. In today's key verse, He declares, "anyone who has looked at me has seen the Father." (John 14:9) And "I only do those things that I see the Father doing." (John 5:19) In other words, we don't have to wonder about God's ways and temperament. Jesus displayed them.

On every day of His earthly ministry, Jesus loved, healed, received, welcomed, forgave, blessed, delivered, and comforted. With the frail and fragile, He was gentle. With the desperate, He was available. With the unlovely, He was kind. With the outcast, He was accepting. He invariably *saw* the ones everyone else overlooked.

Late in his life, John also wrote: "We saw him with our very own eyes. We gazed upon him and heard him speak. Our hands actually touched him, the one who was from the beginning, the Living Expression of God." (1 John 1:1)

At the appearance of the Son of God, the concealing sheet was pulled from the mysterious masterpiece. Through His own life, love, and words, Jesus unveiled a living, breathing image of the God who adopted you and made you His own.

PRAYER OF DECLARATION:

Father, forgive me for ever doubting Your goodness or approaching You as if You are anything other than kind. From this day forward, I will ever be mindful that Jesus clearly displayed Your character and Your values. You long to heal, deliver, rescue, restore, and resurrect. You always have. This is who You are.

An Abundance of Mercy

The faithful love of the Lord never ends!
His mercies never cease.
Great is his faithfulness;
his mercies begin afresh each morning.
LAMENTATIONS 3:22–23 (NLT)

As you undoubtedly recall, the opening days of the emerging Covid-19 pandemic produced a run on (of all things) toilet paper. No one is quite sure why, but over the course of a couple of days, virtually every store shelf on every paper aisle in America was picked clean.

Once the run started, others quickly noticed, and they too joined the great TP panic of 2020. Soon, belief in the shortage of toilet paper became a self-fulfilling outcome. Because people *believed* it to be scarce, it indeed became scarce, for several weeks at least. Only when the myth of the scarcity became apparent did people relax and stop hoarding.

God's grace and mercy are abundant. Yet many believers think, live, and pray as if these extraordinary gifts of God are constantly in short supply. They act as if the sin that draws upon God's forgiveness and grace today somehow leaves less of these in supply for tomorrow's blunder.

In reality, there is no shortage of these precious gifts for all those who are in Christ. God's mercies are inexhaustible. His patience is infinite. No matter how much we draw upon them throughout the day through our mistakes and frailties, each new morning we wake up to find them replenished to overflowing. The truth is, there is no place for a scarcity mentality in anything relating to our infinite, generous, abundant God.

"But won't a belief in the abundance of God's mercy just make me more likely to abuse it?" you may wonder. "Won't it make me more likely to sin and go my own way?"

That's a common fear, but it's simply not how the reborn human heart works. Cultivating a mercy-abundance mentality gives you a more accurate view of the Father who loves you. It will keep you confident in your approach to God's throne. And it will keep you filled with gratitude and tenderness in your relationship with your Father. All of this works together to keep you growing and transforming into the image of Christ.

Oh, daughter of God, it should not surprise you that an infinite God is in possession of infinite quantities of mercy, grace, and patience. And yet, it invariably does, doesn't it? God's wonderfulness never stops startling us. Not only does the "good news" never stop being *good*, it never stops being *news*.

PRAYER OF DECLARATION:

Gracious God, I thank You for the overwhelming abundance of Your mercies. I purpose today to have an abundance mentality where all of Your goodness is concerned. I will access Your grace for every need and every circumstance.

A Good God in a World of Free Choosers

And Yahweh-God commanded him:
"You may freely eat of every fruit of the garden.
But you must not eat of the Tree that gives
the knowledge of good and evil...

GENESIS 2:16–17

We live in a world filled with voices that invite us to question the goodness of God. It seems He's often on trial, standing accused of actively or passively endorsing evil in this world.

For many, a flawed and cartoonish view of God's sovereignty lies at the root of these doubts and accusations. They assume that God is controlling every tiny detail of our world, and therefore must ultimately be personally responsible for all of the tragedy, atrocity, and heartache taking place in it.

This simplistic view doesn't take into account two key things: The first is God's gift of free will to mankind. God granted the first man and woman and all their descendants the freedom to *choose*. The second, often-overlooked key is God's delegation of authority to humanity. The Genesis narrative shows God gifting mankind with legal authority over the entire planet.

Do you see it? God's own righteousness and goodness restrain Him in certain respects from overriding any person's ability to choose life or death, good or evil. What's more, our fallen world is still groaning under the effects of the curse. The world is broken. And so are its people.

Sadly, most believers have been taught a simplistic view of God's sovereignty that ignores both of these realities. It instead assumes that God is getting His way in every moment and place on planet Earth. It's as if Romans 8:28 says, "For we know that God causes all things." It doesn't. It says, "God causes all things to work together for good to those who love Him..." (NASB)

The more-complicated (and more comforting) truth is that our good God is able to constantly factor in the free-will choices of billions of people and still move everything toward the redemptive outcomes He determined long ago. And do so *without* violating our free wills nor the original covenant He made with our fore-parents.

He's *that* smart. He's *that* powerful. And yes, He's *that* good.

This matters immensely because the foundation of your capacity to receive from God is an unshakable confidence that God is good. And it's impossible to reconcile all the hurt, horror, and heartache in the world with the belief that everything always goes exactly as God wants it to. He isn't causing all things. But in love and faithfulness, He is causing all things to work together for your good.

Prayer of Declaration:

Father God, I know the rampant evil, atrocity, and injustice in the world grieves You far more than it does me. Since the day everything went wrong, You have been working relentlessly to make it right again, culminating with the appearance of Your only begotten Son. The One You did not send into the world to condemn it, but to save it. I *choose* to trust in Your goodness.

You Can't Believe Your Eyes

*...because we don't focus our attention on what is seen but on what is unseen.
For what is seen is temporary, but the unseen realm is eternal.*

2 CORINTHIANS 4:18

A dear, wise friend of mine likes to say, "Just because our eyes see all that they see, we assume they see everything there is to see." His point is that there is always more going on around us than we can see, taste, hear, smell, or feel. Even so, believers can spend the bulk of their days focused solely on what their senses are reporting, hardly giving a thought to the fact that much more may be going on unseen all around them.

You're probably aware of the Old Testament story of the servant of the prophet Elisha who woke up to the sight of enemy armies lining the hillsides all around him—and panicked. Elisha's helper thought the prophet was crazy for being calm...right up to the moment his spiritual eyes were opened.

Only then could he see the overwhelming multitude of angelic help that was present to fight on their behalf. You see, our natural senses can never tell us the whole truth. Paul had these angelic armies and other unseen realities in mind when he wrote, concerning Christ:

> For in him was created the universe of things, both in the heavenly realm and on the earth, all that is seen and all that is unseen. Every seat of power, realm of government, principality,

and authority—it all exists through him and for his purpose!
(Colossians 1:16)

Not only are our senses incomplete, but they're also unreliable. They are easily fooled. Our eyes can and do literally deceive us. That's why the believer who follows Paul's advice in today's key verse and keeps her focus on "unseen" things isn't "in denial," or engaging in wishful thinking, when she refuses to panic and freak out when the visible circumstances seem grim.

Know that the natural evidence is not *all the evidence*. In fact, the natural evidence is actually less reliable and more transient than the spiritual realities governed by God's Word and backed by His character. Or, in Paul's words in today's key verse, one is "temporary" while the other is "eternal."

Finally, as you pray, keep in mind that the natural world bends to the authority of the spiritual. This principle is at the root of every miracle recorded in the Bible. Don't rely solely on what your natural senses observe. Don't evaluate your circumstances only on what you see. You can't believe your natural eyes alone. And don't make the mistake of thinking that when you pray and don't immediately see change, that nothing is happening.

PRAYER OF DECLARATION:

Holy Spirit of God, as I move through my days, keep me mindful that there is far more going on around me than my natural senses can perceive. Help me glimpse and understand the spiritual truth and realities in every circumstance. I'll esteem Your Word and character more highly than my fallible, foolable senses.

Liberated from Self-Consciousness

God is love! Those who are living in love are living in God, and God lives through them... Our love for others is our grateful response to the love God first demonstrated to us.

1 JOHN 4:16B,19

You're about to walk into a room filled with strangers. You take a deep breath. Your thoughts swirl. *What will they think of me? Will they like me? Will they approve of me? How will I compare to them?* Welcome to the all-too familiar bondage of self-consciousness.

Here's wonderful news. A revelation of how loved and accepted you are in Christ is one of the most liberating things you can experience. Believers who come to fully grasp and understand the goodness and grace of God suddenly find themselves free to think about others.

It carries the power to free the human soul from one of the cruelest forms of slavery—the bondage of self-consciousness. The 19th-century Scottish preacher Alexander MacLaren once wrote: "The very essence of love is that it looks away from itself. Love brings an end to the tormenting, anxious thought of 'What will become of me?' God's love frees me in one sweep from all the torturing anxieties and trembling fears of *self*-consciousness."

This is the freedom Jesus both walked in and displayed every day of His earthly ministry. We never read of Him entering a room occupied with concerns about what others thought of Him. We never see Him wracked by insecurity or compelled by the need for approval. When Jesus entered a crowded room, all of His attention was on the Spirit who was showing Him the needs and wounds of others.

You were reborn to live this way as well, but it requires a revelation of God's love and faithfulness. Such a revelation is precisely what Paul prayed for the believers at Ephesus to receive—that they would be "rooted and grounded in love." (Ephesians 3:17 ESV) And that as a result, they would come "to know the love of Christ which surpasses knowledge, that you may be filled up to all the fullness of God." (vv. 18–19 NASB)

Sink the roots of your awareness deeply into that love and draw it into you right now. Let the deep rootedness anchor you solidly in your true identity: "Daughter of God." You are only free to become others-oriented and joyfully unselfish when you understand how completely and unconditionally you are loved by God. And you are!

You can and will be free from the torment and timidity of self-consciousness.

PRAYER OF DECLARATION:

Father, Your Holy Spirit is opening my eyes to the depth, height, and breadth of Your love for me. You're rooting and grounding me in it, freeing me from the slavery of self-consciousness. I'm free! Free to forget me. Free to see others and love them with Your love.

Escape the Funhouse

Help, Lord! Save us! For godly ones are disappearing.
Where are the dependable, principled ones? They're a vanishing breed!
Everyone lies, everyone flatters, and everyone deceives.
Nothing but empty talk, smooth talk, and double-talk.

PSALM 12:1–2

Have you ever been inside an old-school carnival "funhouse?" The kind with a maze of strange mirrors and optical illusions specially designed to trick and confuse you? Some mirrors make you look impossibly round. Others twist you into a bizarre hourglass or other shapes. Clusters of mirrors disorient you. Other rooms with tilted floors and angled walls toy with your sense of balance.

Doesn't that sound like "fun?" No? Well, it seems, thanks to the internet and social media, we've all entered a type of global funhouse. Traditional, long-trusted sources of news and information have abandoned any pretense of objectivity and now simply serve as propaganda arms for one side or another in the "culture wars."

Thirty years ago, our sources of information came from a mere handful of large media organizations operating exclusively in three realms: television, radio, and print. For better and worse, the internet and smartphones upended all of that. Today every individual on the planet is a "news source" and a pundit, offering opinions, perspectives, and interpretations of the news—often anonymously and therefore with NO accountability. Many have an axe to grind, a viewpoint to sell, a grudge to settle, or a cause to advance. Some deliberately lie. Many unwittingly share false information with their network of friends.

Perhaps the psalmist David prophetically saw our predicament when he wrote his cry of "Help, Lord!" to begin today's key scripture passage. In a funhouse environment, you can't trust your own eyes. In a similar way, you can't even trust your own brain because of something psychologists call cognitive biases. For example, confirmation bias causes you to notice "facts" that harmonize with what you already believe while making you generally blind to information that contradicts that belief.

So, is there any good news here? Yes! David delivers it in verse six of the same chapter as today's key passage: "For every word Yahweh speaks is sure and reliable. His truth is tested, found to be flawless, and ever faithful. It's as pure as silver refined seven times in a crucible of clay." (Psalm 12:6)

You have a sure, reliable, trustworthy, ever-present source of information and guidance living right inside of you: the Holy Spirit of God. "The Helper," Jesus called Him. More trustworthy than your own perceptions and thought processes, He is your way out of the funhouse.

PRAYER OF DECLARATION:

The Holy Spirit is my Helper; I shall not be deceived. Today and every day I turn my attention away from the flattery, lies, and deceit of this world's information systems and toward the faithful flawless Words of my God. I trust in Him and do not lean to my own understanding.

The Ultimate Security System

I give to them the gift of eternal life and they will never be lost and no one has the power to snatch them out of my hands. My Father, who has given them to me as his gift, is the mightiest of all, and no one has the power to snatch them from my Father's care.

JOHN 10:28–29

It now stands as one of the most famous kidnapping cases in U.S. history. In a series of events that represent pretty much every young girl's darkest fear, 14-year-old Elizabeth Smart was kidnapped at knifepoint from her own bed by an intruder on the night of June 5, 2002. She was rescued nine months later. In the years since, Smart has endeavored to redeem her nightmarish ordeal by becoming an advocate for victims of sexual assault and for missing children.

Many Christian women live with a related *spiritual* fear. Namely, that somehow, they will be snatched from the comfort and love of their place in God's household. That they will do something wrong that results in their losing their place at God's bountiful banquet table of grace.

Your enemy—who, you may remember, Jesus called "the father of lies" (John 8:44)—loves to try to rob you of the joy and confidence of your salvation. In fact, since Jesus stripped him of his authority through His victory over death. Lies are really the only remaining weapon in the devil's arsenal.

One of the most common lies is the notion that you should live in ongoing fear of God's judgment. That God may become so annoyed with your mistakes and failings, He may eventually abandon you or reject you altogether. Or you might somehow disqualify yourself from His protection, leaving yourself vulnerable to "kidnap" by God's mortal enemy. Nothing could be further from the truth.

Jesus made it clear: When you repent of your sins and place your faith in Him, you are *forever* His, and nothing—including your own human frailty and fallibility—can remove you from His hand. You have passed from death to life and out of the fear of judgment forever.

The startling truth of today's key scripture is this: YOU were a gift from God to His Son. That's right. God gave Jesus *you* as a present. And both are mighty enough to keep such a precious gift safe. Their security system is more than up to the task of keeping you right where you belong. No, the enemy can't have you. But by getting you to believe a lie, he can rob you of one of the key parts of your birthright as a daughter of God—your peace and sense of security.

You belong to Him now. And nothing, not even your own periodic foolishness, can remove you from His mighty, loving hand. This is settled forever.

PRAYER OF DECLARATION:

Jesus, I belong to You, having been given to You as a gift of love from the Father. I am secure and at rest, and therefore free to follow wherever You lead. I am in the Father's care, and nothing, not even my own occasional willfulness, can take me from His mighty hands.

Fearless Living

For God will never give you the spirit of fear,
but the Holy Spirit who gives you
mighty power, love, and self-control.

2 Timothy 1:7

The world has experienced a lot of shaking and disruption recently. But we are far from the first generation to go through something like this. Between 1914 and 1918 the world experienced a global war and a global pandemic—both of which combined to produce massive economic turmoil. World War I killed roughly 20 million people while the "Spanish Flu" is estimated to have killed between 50 and 100 million people (roughly 3% of all people on earth.)

A little more than 100 years later, the fear and anxiety many are feeling are real and palpable. Our great-grandparents went through a lot, but they didn't have to contend with the amplifying, distorting effects of the internet and social media. Today we're constantly bombarded with troubling, often terrifying, information and images. All of this points to one thing…

This is the perfect time to learn to walk in faith and peace rather than fear and anxiety. But how?

As anyone who has battled fear can tell you, this beast doesn't respond to reason. You can't simply tell a fear-filled person to just stop being fearful. Providing facts and logic is futile. A spiritual condition can't be fixed by feeding the mind. It can only be eradicated by a Spirit-encounter with Love personified.

This is why Paul's prayer for his friends in Ephesus (and you) was: "…that you, being rooted and established in love, may have power, together with all the Lord's holy people, to grasp how wide and long and high and deep is the love of Christ, and to know this love that surpasses knowledge—that you may be filled to the measure of all the fullness of God." (Ephesians 3:17–19 NIV)

The more you immerse yourself and anchor your heart in the truth of Jesus' boundless, unconditional love for you, the less fear plays a part in your life. This is vital because fear is a spiritual force. In a sense, it is the opposite of faith. Faith is a positive expectancy of good from God; fear is a negative expectancy. As such, it shuts down our capacity to receive from God. What a hellish prison it is to live in fear.

This need not be true for you. You can be, in Paul's words, "rooted and established in love" as you immerse yourself and anchor your heart in the truth of Jesus' boundless, unconditional love for you. The God of the Universe has placed His covenant love upon you. You are encircled with the strong, loving arms of a faithful Father. The Lord is your Light and Salvation. Whom shall you fear?

Prayer of Declaration:

Dear God, by Your Spirit, grace me with a fresh revelation of Your love for me. I come into agreement with Paul's Ephesians Three prayer: Let the knowledge of Your boundless, unconditional love for me drive out any-and-all remnants of fear from my soul—filling me with the fullness of You. I expect good because I am Yours.

The Illusion of Control

He's the hope that holds me and the stronghold to shelter me,
the only God for me, and my great confidence.
He will rescue you from every hidden trap of the enemy,
and he will protect you from false accusation and any deadly curse.
His massive arms are wrapped around you, protecting you.
You can run under his covering of majesty and hide.
His arms of faithfulness are a shield keeping you from harm.

PSALM 91:2—4

Here's a true statement you may struggle to accept. The world is *not* a more dangerous place than ever before. It simply isn't. The hard, objective data makes that clear. Yet it doesn't *feel* that way, does it? That's because we live immersed in media driven by a 24-hour "bad-news" cycle.

Our constant connection to media is like an intravenous drip of terrifying reports and images. *Drip, drip, drip.* With each alarming drop, our anxiety rises and our sense of safety sinks lower. On top of this, many of us have experienced real trauma in the past—often when we were young. This tends to result in some fierce inner vows: *I will never be blindsided like that again. I will be vigilant. I will see it coming.* Such vows produce two things in you:

First, you constantly scan the horizon for threats. You frantically do research from a deeply flawed belief that the more you *know*, the safer you'll be. But knowing more doesn't make you safer. It does, however, make you more fearful.

Secondly, that fear produces a frantic quest to control everything in your environment—including the people who live in it. You believe that if you can exert enough control over your circumstances and the people around you, you can keep yourself and them safe. Far too many of God's precious daughters are living their lives this way. Perhaps you are one of them.

Here's the truth about that belief: The relentless, fear-driven quest for control is both fruitless and counterproductive. Not only is it impossible, but it also makes you and everyone around you miserable—draining life of joy and peace. What's worse, it removes from the equation the very One who *can* control what concerns you and keep you and your loved ones secure. That's your loving heavenly Father there in today's key passage. (Go back and read it again.)

Now read the words of Romans 8:28–29a: "So we are convinced that every detail of our lives is continually woven together for good, for we are his lovers who have been called to fulfill his designed purpose. For he knew all about us before we were born and he destined us from the beginning to share the likeness of his Son."

Control is an illusion. What is real is God's care and His power to cause everything to result in your good. So, renounce the old vows. Shift your confidence from your own puny ability to foresee danger to the massive arms that are right now wrapped around you in protective love.

Prayer of Declaration:

Father, Your arms of faithfulness are a shield keeping me from harm. Under the protective covering of Your majesty, I enjoy rest and find peace. I don't have to scan the horizon because You know the future. In Your immense power and love, You are continually weaving everything together into a tapestry of "good" for me.

When God Introduces Himself

The Lord passed in front of Moses, calling out,
"Yahweh! The Lord! The God of compassion and mercy!
I am slow to anger and filled with unfailing love and faithfulness.
I lavish unfailing love to a thousand generations.
I forgive iniquity, rebellion, and sin"

EXODUS 34:6—7 NLT

There's an old saying: "First impressions are lasting impressions." You've also probably heard the related maxim, "You never get a second chance to make a first impression." Both are true. Which is why introductions are important.

How you introduce yourself to someone says so much about you. It reveals what you think is most important for the other party to know about you.

Did you know the Bible records the moment God reintroduced Himself to mankind? We know that Adam and Eve originally enjoyed an intimate friendship with their Creator. We also know the fall of Mankind dropped a thick, isolating curtain between God and people. With Moses, God began the slow, methodical process of restoring that connection.

That moment of introduction took place as God was delivering the ten commandments to him. You see, in ancient times, a visiting king from another realm would be announced by a "herald" before he entered the room. The herald would go before the king, shout the monarch's name, and announce some of his most important attributes. This often included the size of his armies, how many nations he had conquered, and the vastness of his wealth.

God—alone with Moses on the cloud-shrouded heights of Sinai—has no herald, so He does the job Himself. That moment is recorded in today's key scripture. God shouts His own name, "Yahweh! The Lord!" Now please notice what God chooses to cite as His defining characteristics when introducing Himself:

Compassion. Mercy. Slowness to anger. Unfailing love. Faithful. Forgiving.

Daughter of God, *this* is how God reintroduced Himself to His beloved-but-estranged creation. This is what He felt was most important for humanity—and you—to know. If those terms don't align with your primary conception of the God who chose you to be His own, you likely have some mind-renewal work to do. (It's okay, most of us do.)

Here is the extraordinary, liberating truth: You belong to a God of unspeakable kindness and compassion. He is a wonderful Father. When the Creator of the Universe tells you what He's like...believe Him!

PRAYER OF DECLARATION:

Father forgive me for ever doubting Your goodness or approaching You as if You were anything other than kind. You are compassionate, merciful, and slow to anger. Your love is unfailing. Your faithfulness is unwavering. You love to forgive and delight in restoring. So, I come to You with a heart filled with gladness, gratitude, and expectancy.

Your Prince on a White Horse

*Then I saw heaven opened, and suddenly a white horse appeared.
The name of the one riding it was Faithful and True,
and with pure righteousness he judges and rides to battle.*

REVELATION 19:11

It's a timeworn Hollywood cliché, isn't it? The brave prince charges in on a white horse to rescue the lovely but poor maiden in her moment of peril. They ride off together to build a blissful life. Of course, Hollywood clichés don't survive to become such if they don't speak to something that resonates within the hearts of a lot of people.

Here's the truth: we're *all* in desperate need of rescue. Every man and woman on the planet needs a hero to pull us out of the hopeless circumstances into which we're all born. There are no exceptions. The rich and powerful; the poor and oppressed; the up-and-coming and the down-and-out. We're all helpless and doomed, unless…

The full title of the book of Revelation is "The Revelation of Jesus Christ." There we find a striking image of the risen King. Here we have the reigning, ruling King Jesus leading His Kingdom armies forth as they make His enemies—sickness, oppression, injustice, lack, and all the other effects of the curse—a footstool for His feet. Yet in this fiercely vivid description, the first thing we learn of this awe-inspiring rider on a white horse is what He is called:

Faithful and True.

What a wonderful thing to keep in mind as you follow your Savior-King day by day, moment by moment. Never lose sight of the truth that the hero who rode to your rescue, compelled by fierce love and compassion, has two key attributes above all others.

First, the One into whose hands you have placed your life is *faithful*. He will never leave you nor forsake you. He called Himself "the Good Shepherd who lays down my life as a sacrifice for the sheep." (John 10:11) He is the one with a love so great that He lays down His life for His friends. (John 15:13)

Second, you should never lose touch with the reality that the object of your worship is *true*. He cannot deceive. He will not lie. His words are Spirit and life (John 6:63), and you can rest your full weight upon them with utter confidence. He initiated your journey of faith by choosing and rescuing you, and you can count on His promise to see it through. (Hebrews 12:2)

We know how this love story ends. It's a happy-ever-after eternity. Between now and then, we'll enjoy far greater levels of peace and power if we'll simply keep in mind the name of that Rider on a white horse who plucked us out of a hopeless, dark fate. The One who rode to save you is called "Faithful and True."

Prayer of Declaration:

Jesus, my Faithful and True Champion, I put the full weight of my trust and confidence in You today. I know every word You have spoken to me is true. You have pledged yourself to me and to the process of transforming me into Your own image. So, I am at peace. I know You are leading me to victory. Your victory.

Showered in Grace,
Wrapped in Favor

For it was always in his perfect plan to adopt us as his delightful children,
through our union with Jesus, the Anointed One, so that his tremendous love
that cascades over us would glorify his grace—for the same love he has for the
Beloved, Jesus, he has for us. And this unfolding plan brings him great pleasure!

EPHESIANS 1:6

Have you ever stood under a waterfall in some exotic tropical locale? It's an exhilarating experience. Stepping back from the curtain of falling water feels like entering a strange secret world. Stepping forward into the downpour immerses you completely in sound and sensation.

In today's key verse, Paul reveals the Father's brilliant plan to bring us into His family involved pouring out a "tremendous love that cascades over us," like a waterfall. There is a single Greek word lying beneath that lovely phrase: *charitoo*.

It's a wonderful word that shares a root with the words *charis* and *charisma*. These are usually translated as "grace" and connote "a gift." They show up many times in the New Testament. But *charitoo* only appears in one other place.

When the angel Gabriel appeared to Mary to let her know she was about to conceive the Messiah, he greeted her by calling her *charitoo!* (Luke 1:28) In that passage, many translators render that greeting "highly favored." *The Passion Translation* has the angel telling Mary she has been "*anointed* with great favor." Anointed is an apt word because *charitoo* suggests a liberal "pouring out" of grace and favor. This is why we see the word "cascades" in Ephesians 1:6. Another definition of *charitoo* is "to be compassed, or surrounded, with favor."

Indeed, the psalmist David seems to have had *charitoo* in mind when he wrote: "Lord, how wonderfully you bless the righteous. Your favor wraps around each one and covers them under your canopy of kindness and joy." (Psalm 5:12) Of course, some will read this promise and immediately disqualify themselves. *Oh, I'm not righteous*, they instantly think.

Beloved daughter of God, that simply isn't true. Through your "union with Jesus," you have been made righteous with His righteousness. (2 Corinthians 5:21) In Him, you are *charitoo*—gifted with a never-ending outpouring of love, grace, and favor.

By faith, incorporate the astonishing truth of today's key verse deep into your sense of identity. *Believe* what God's Word is saying—that it was always God's plan to adopt you by merging you with His Son. Know that His inexhaustible grace constantly pours down upon you as if you were standing beneath a waterfall. His favor has you surrounded. You're wrapped in it.

Prayer of Declaration:

Father, You have called me *charitoo*—highly favored, standing under cascades of Your love and wrapped securely in Your heavenly favor. Who am I to argue with You? Because You have made me righteous with Jesus' righteousness, I move through this day under a protective canopy of Your goodness. I will live in the quiet confidence that comes from the assurance that Your favor encircles me.

IV. Grace for Breakthrough

Not for Sale

For by grace you have been saved by faith. Nothing you did could ever earn
this salvation, for it was the love gift from God that brought us to Christ!
So no one will ever be able to boast, for salvation is never a reward
for good works or human striving.

EPHESIANS 2:8—9

We're transactional creatures by nature and by training. We're
conditioned from birth to view everything in terms of an
exchange. We earn dessert for eating our veggies. We get an
allowance for doing chores. Merchandise for money. Wages for
work. Value for comparable value.

We're comfortable with that because there's a part of us that
likes to feel we've earned what we've received. This explains why
we tend to feel so uncomfortable when someone surprises us
with a gift when we have nothing in return to give them.

It's humbling. And something deeply embedded in our old,
fallen nature doesn't want to be humbled. It's no accident that
pride drove both Lucifer's fall and the very first human sin.

This also explains why so many of God's people struggle to
receive and experience the fullness of what Jesus died to provide
for them. Relationship with God does not operate transactionally, even though we often treat Him as if it does. We think, *If I
do good* for *God, I'll get good* from *God.* That's not living faith; that's
lifeless religion.

God does not ask us to pay an admission price. He simply bids us to come as we are. Jesus once depicted the kingdom of His Father as a feast to which messengers canvassed the highways and side streets, imploring everyone to come and dine. A place at the table is not for sale. It is freely offered to "whosoever will." The great South African preacher and prayer warrior, Andrew Murray (1828–1917), once wrote:

> Faith—simple faith in God's word and love—results in the opening of the eyes, the opening of the heart, to receive and enjoy the unspeakable glory of His grace. And just as the trees, day by day, and month by month, stand and grow into beauty and fruitfulness by just welcoming whatever sunshine the sun may give, so the highest form of the Christian life is just to abide in the light of God. And to let that light, to let *Him*, fill you with the life and the brightness it brings.

As the trees welcome the gift of sunlight and naturally turn it into green growth and fruit, we are called to receive His grace, to abide in His light, to let Him fill us with life. We cannot earn it. Nor does He ask us to try. *Just receive. Abide. Let Him do what He does.*

PRAYER OF DECLARATION:

Gracious Father, I will not insult You or Your great grace by attempting to "buy" with my meager means what You have offered as a wildly extravagant gift. I humbly and gratefully open my arms to receive what You long to give. Like a tree, my growth and fruitfulness come not from straining or striving but from simply soaking in the light of Your Presence and the rain of Your goodness.

Where Power Rushes In

But he [the Lord] answered me, "My grace is always more than enough for you, and my power finds its full expression through your weakness." So I will celebrate my weaknesses, for when I'm weak I sense more deeply the mighty power of Christ living in me.

2 Corinthians

"I do it myself!" Everyone who has ever parented a three-year-old knows this refrain well. In their path of development, every child ultimately reaches an age in which they no longer want mom or dad to do things for them. They want the satisfaction of doing things on their own. This is a healthy and natural part of growing up. Most of us bring a similar impulse into our growing up in God. But it's not nearly as healthy.

We prefer to take things as far as possible in our own strength, ability, and "wisdom." Well-meaning voices in our lives even encourage this. "God helps those who help themselves," we're assured.

Often, it is only when we reach the end of our own natural capacity that we are willing to call on God for help. It's only when our brilliant plans go tragically wrong or when our tight grip of control on our circumstances gets slippery that we start to send up distress flares for help from God.

Of course, as with audacious, water-walking Peter rapidly sinking beneath the waves, our gracious Saviour is ever-ready to reach out and rescue us. But why wait until we come to the end of ourselves? Why not just live in recognition that we're *always* at the end of ourselves? Why not live in constant connection to His power?

A faithful paraphrase of today's key verse would have the Father saying to you: "My grace is all you need because in every area in which you recognize that you're weak, My supernatural power rushes in to carry you." That's the key. *Recognizing* and admitting your need. It requires laying aside the toddler impulse of "I do it myself!"

It is one thing to know that God is willing and able to carry you through your trials—great and small—but something completely different to *let* Him. Jesus once looked at an entire city and said, "So many times I have longed to gather a wayward people, as a hen gathers her chicks under her wings—but you were too stubborn to let me." (Matthew 23:37)

That same Redeemer described the Holy Spirit as "the Helper." Shockingly the only barrier to living in a constant state of supernatural help is your own pride. His gracious invitation is that you "cast all your cares upon Him" in calm confidence that He cares for you. (1 Peter 5:7 NIV) Humility and a heart of gratitude are the twin keys to a lifestyle of power-filled rest.

Prayer of Declaration:

Father, I can't do it myself. I just can't. I'm weak and frail and in desperate need of You, moment by moment. I recognize that I'm always at the end of myself. But Your grace—Your unmerited gift of power and strength—is oh so much more than enough for me.

If You Only Knew Who…
You Would Ask

She replied, "Why would a Jewish man ask a Samaritan woman for a drink of water?" (For Jews have no dealings with Samaritans.) Jesus replied, "If you only knew who I am and the gift that God wants to give you, you'd ask me for a drink, and I would give you living water."

JOHN 4:9–10

Most of the women of this Samaritan village came here to the well much earlier this morning to draw the day's water before the sun made the journey unbearably hot. They came in a group both for safety and conversation. But now, in the heat at midday, a woman approaches the well alone.

As she rounds a corner in the path, she is startled to see a solitary man sitting in the shade of a tree beside the well. She freezes and quickly assesses the situation. She is alone and vulnerable. She doesn't recognize the man, and his manner of clothing presents a second shock. He is not Samaritan but Jewish.

Suddenly, a third surprise. The man breaks the tense silence by politely asking for a drink of water. She knows very well that, in doing so, this man with the kind voice had violated both deeply entrenched cultural convention and Jewish law. Smart, feisty, and hardened by a life filled with hard choices and hard men, she decides to challenge him about the long-festering theological disagreement sitting at the center of the hatred between the Jews and her people.

She wants to debate…but this stranger wants to give her a new and better life. Look again at Jesus' response to this woman's challenge found in today's key verse: "If you only knew *who I am* and the gift that God wants to give you, *you'd ask me* for a drink, and *I would give* you living water." Do you see it?

If you only knew Who… You would have asked… And He would have given…

Intrigued, the woman asked Jesus to explain this mysterious "living water." His answer: "*If you drink from Jacob's well, you'll be thirsty again, but if anyone drinks the living water I give them, they will never be thirsty again. For when you drink the water I give you, it becomes a gushing fountain of the Holy Spirit, flooding you with endless life!*" (John 4:13–14)

What was true for that precious woman is true for you today. The more you come to understand *Who* died for you—the enormity of His love, the comprehensiveness of what He purchased for you on the cross—the bolder and bigger you will *ask* of Him.

Today, and every day, you can find yourself standing face-to-face with the One who gives living water, and with it, every other good and perfect thing. If you have eyes to see Who He really is, you'll ask…and He will give…freely and abundantly.

PRAYER OF DECLARATION:

Jesus, I know who it is I'm speaking to right now. You're my gracious Savior and King, So, I'm asking big and boldly of You today. Having glimpsed Your authority and character, I'm asking You for a fresh drink of the living water only You can give.

Dance with the One
Who Brought You

So answer me this: Did the Holy Spirit come to you as a reward for keeping Jewish laws? No, you received him as a gift because you believed in the Messiah. Your new life began when the Holy Spirit gave you a new birth. Why then would you so foolishly turn from living in the Spirit by trying to finish by your own works?

GALATIANS 3:2–3

There's an old saying from the rural, deep south along the lines of, "You ought to dance with the one what brung you."

In case you need a translation from the original vernacular, the reference is to a girl who accepts an invitation to a dance from a gentleman, but when she arrives with him, proceeds to dance with other guys at the ball. The lesson at the heart of the saying is that it's both wise and prudent to stick with the methods and modes that got you where you are in the first place.

Paul seems to have had this principle in mind when he told the believers in Colossae, "So then, just as you received Christ Jesus as Lord, continue to live your lives in him." (Colossians 2:6 NIV) And how did we receive Jesus? "By grace, through faith," as Paul reminds us in Ephesians 2:8–9 (NIV).

Paul practically shouted this same principle in his letter to the believers in Galatia. With more than a bit of exasperation in his tone, he wrote the words of today's key verse. Paraphrasing Paul in modern terms:

> "Look guys, you received this whole new journey in God through the work of the Holy Spirit. Do you seriously now think that you're going to get the rest of the way through your own efforts? It began as a free gift. But now you're going to earn and merit and obey your way to the finish line? Really? (Had it been available, Paul might have used the facepalm emoji here.)

Paul's warnings about these things in his writings are both frequent and forceful, precisely because the temptation for believers to dance with "works" and "performance" is so very powerful. The dance partners "earn" and "merit" and "deserve" flatter our pride and soulish craving for self-sufficiency. So, we leave the kind and loyal One who brought us to the ball—the Spirit of grace—and waltz off with these flattering but empty suitors.

The grace and mercy of a compassionate Savior wooed you by His Spirit and, when you said "yes" to His invitation, miraculously transferred you from the domain of darkness to a kingdom of light and life and love. Now you're at the dance of eternity. Dance with the One who brought you.

Prayer of Declaration:

Spirit of Grace, thank You for bringing me to the ball of eternal life in Jesus. How gracious of You to invite me, to woo me. What a gift! I receive it with humility and gratitude. Now that I'm here, I hear the invitations to dance with "earn," "merit," and "deserve," but I will decline their advances. You brought me here. You and You alone can carry me all the way home.

The Ultimate
Wardrobe Upgrade

You have all become true children of God by faith in Jesus Christ!
Faith immersed you into Christ,
and now you are covered and clothed with his life.

GALATIANS 3:26–27

If it seems that a new outfit, or a new handbag and shoes, can make you feel different about yourself, it's not your imagination. A 2016 psychology experiment by researchers at Penn State University found that when people temporarily upgraded their work wardrobe with more-expensive designer labels they not only felt more confident but actually performed better. (They even got better at solving math problems!)

Let's shift that idea from the natural to the spiritual. One of the most powerful, life-transforming, confidence-building things you can do is come to understand that when you gave your life to Jesus, you became *clothed* in Him. That's the stunning news embedded in today's key verse.

The miraculous event of the new birth simultaneously immerses you into Jesus AND fills you with Him. That's one of the magnificent, mysterious truths about the salvation experience. It creates a state of being for the believer in which we are simultaneously in Jesus, even as He is in us.

This truth is emphasized and reiterated over and over in the New Testament, both in the words of Jesus and in the letters of Paul and John. In just the first chapter of Ephesians alone, you'll find roughly a dozen occurrences of phrases like "in Him," "in Christ," and "in Christ Jesus."

The full witness of the New Covenant is this: Because we are in Jesus and He in us, we are "clothed" in His righteousness, His favor, and His authority. That is our legal position in the courts of heaven. This means that you never come to God in prayer as yourself alone. You can approach God's throne boldly and confidently precisely because you come "in Jesus" and with Him in you. And because you come in His righteousness, His favor, and His authority, you qualify for every one of the great and precious promises in the Word.

When your heart becomes deeply convinced of this truth, the gratitude, joy, and adoration this produces propels your worship to new heights. And the confidence this produces fuels your faith to receive miracles—for others and for yourself. You will run boldly and confidently to God's throne when you know you are in Jesus, and Jesus is in you.

You'll know you are just as received, welcomed, and favored as is God's own beloved Son. That's quite a wardrobe upgrade.

Prayer of Declaration:

I come into the courts of heaven today clothed in Jesus' righteousness, favor, and authority. Father, You've clothed me in Your flawless Son. That means I walk in this world as Christ's image bearer and that I wield both His authority and His power as I move through my day. I declare that in Him I stand fully qualified to receive every good and perfect gift from Your gracious hand.

Discover Your Superpower

I pray that you will continually experience the immeasurable greatness of God's power made available to you through faith. Then your lives will be an advertisement of this immense power as it works through you! This is the mighty power that was released when God raised Christ from the dead and exalted him to the place of highest honor and supreme authority in the heavenly realm!

EPHESIANS 1:19–20

It raked in more than $822 million in box office receipts world-wide. In 2017's *Wonder Woman*, former Israeli soldier Gal Gadot captured the imaginations of girls all over the planet with her combination of compassion for the vulnerable and extraordinary power...superpower, actually.

In this fallen, broken world, power—particularly spiritual power—can come in mighty handy. It can rescue your loved ones, save the day for your family, carry you through adversity, and cause good to triumph over evil.

Have you ever asked God for more spiritual power? If so, ponder for a moment the mind-blowing implications of today's key passage of scripture. Buried deep in the truth-rich recesses of Ephesians' extraordinary first chapter, those two verses speak of "the incredible greatness of God's power for us" and then link that power directly to the immense force that not only raised Jesus from the dead but also enthroned Him at God's right hand.

Look closely at those verses one more time. Who is this power directed toward? It is "for us"…those of us who believe Him. This power is not reserved for those who have earned it through good behavior and extra good works. It has not been set aside as a special reward for an elite class of super-Christians. This power is for you, daughter of God.

Simple belief is the only stated qualification here. As with almost every other blessing and benefit in God's remarkable Kingdom of Grace, childlike acceptance in faith is the key to everything. "Only believe," Jesus told the heartbroken Jairus who had just heard that his little daughter had died. (Mark 5:36 NASB)

That remains His request of us today. Unimaginable heavenly power is waiting to be deployed in you and for you. Only believe.

Paul prayed for the Ephesians to have a fuller understanding of the divine power that was available to them. Perhaps you should ask this for yourself today. Ask the Spirit to open the eyes of your understanding. Increase your faith. Then choose, with the faith of a little child, to simply believe.

You may just find yourself in the role of a new kind of superhero.

PRAYER OF DECLARATION:

Oh Father, how incredibly great is Your power in me and for me! I declare that the same mighty power that raised Christ from the dead and seated Him in the place of honor at Your right hand in the heavenly realms is now flowing to me to advance Your Kingdom and to accomplish everything that concerns me. I believe!

Are You in "Airplane Mode?"

Everything we could ever need for life and godliness has already been deposited in us by his divine power. For all this was lavished upon us through the rich experience of knowing him who has called us by name and invited us to come to him through a glorious manifestation of his goodness.

2 PETER 1:3

These days we hold our entire lives in the palms of our hands. We manage our schedules there. Our entertainment world is there, as is control of our homes and finances. For better or worse, (mostly worse) our relationships are maintained there, too. We've become accustomed to instantly getting the answer to every little question that pops into our minds. *What was the name of that guy who was in that movie about that spy thing?*

Of course, I'm talking about our smartphones. We've become dependent upon them in countless ways. Yet they're useless without connectivity to either a cellular network or WiFi. If you've ever found yourself without either "bars" or a WiFi signal, you will likely recall the rising, panicky sense of helplessness at the dawning awareness of how much you rely on your phone minute by minute. The struggle for WiFi is real.

Of course, wireless signals are invisible. Completely undetectable by our senses. So how do we know they're there? How could you prove the existence of these intangible impulses to a skeptic? It's quite simple. You could just pick up your phone and demonstrate access to what is being provided. The evidence would be music, images, information, new emails, and directions.

Something very similar is true where the promises of God are concerned. If you are in Christ and He is in you, all of God's promises belong to you. That's the glorious, reassuring truth in today's key verse. God is constantly and faithfully transmitting two kinds of good things to you. Things that pertain to "life" and "godliness." In other words, both *natural* things (life) and *spiritual* things (godliness). That covers everything!

God is good and faithful to provide the signal—because His covenant commitment is actually not to us but to His Son. We get what Jesus deserves because we're "in Him." So, if we're not seeing that flow of provision, the problem must be on our side. This happens when you take your eyes off of Jesus and His finished work on your behalf and put them on yourself. You move your focus from His perfection to your imperfection. When you do this, it's like putting your phone into "airplane mode."

Of course, the enemy of your soul—"the accuser of the brethren"—is always ready to assist in this self-defeating process. Don't shut off your WiFi. Keep focused on "the rich experience of knowing Him who has called you by name."

Prayer of Declaration:

Father, because of Jesus, You have already provided and are constantly transmitting to me everything I need to thrive both naturally and spiritually. All of this was lavished upon me through the rich experience of knowing Jesus. I will not turn off my capacity to receive from You by putting my eyes on my imperfect self. Jesus, my eyes are on You. I'm connected. I'm receiving.

Come Into Agreement with God

The voice spoke again. "Nothing is unclean if God declares it to be clean."
ACTS 10:15

Are you holy? Ask the typical believer that question and you'll likely hear an awkward silence followed by some disclaimers followed by a stammered response that ranges somewhere between "not really" and "heavens, no!" Ask, "Are you pure?" and the responses will be equally sheepish.

These answers come in spite of the fact that the Word of God is clear and emphatic. If you are in Christ, God has declared you holy, clean, and pure. First Corinthians 6:11 couldn't be more transparent on this issue: *"...but now you have been purified from sin, made holy, and given a perfect standing before God—all because of the power of the name of the Lord Jesus, the Messiah, and through our union with the Spirit of our God."*

Why do we doubt the truth of this? It's that we know ourselves too well. We know the thoughts that cross our minds when we feel angry, offended, or slighted. We know the vivid stories that privately play themselves out upon the movie screens of our imaginations. We know what we'd be capable of if there were no accountability in our lives.

This is why we're much more likely to nod in agreement with Jeremiah 17:9 ("The heart is deceitful above all things, and desperately wicked..." KJV) than with Hebrews 10:10 ("...we have been purified and made holy once and for all through the sacrifice of the body of Jesus…").

Very early in the life of the Church, the Apostle Peter had a remarkable vision that completely altered the course of Christian history. In the tenth chapter of Acts, we read how the former fisherman was praying on a rooftop when he saw heaven opened up and a sheet descending before him. On that sheet were many animals that the Levitical dietary laws declared unclean.

As a devout Jewish follower of Jesus, Peter instantly recognized these creatures as forbidden and defiling to even touch. Thus, he was shocked to hear a voice from heaven commanding him to kill and eat them! Of course, Peter protested. In response, the voice of the Lord issued the command contained in today's Scripture verse: "Nothing is unclean if God declares it to be clean."

The Spirit of God could very well say the same thing to us today. God has declared you righteous. Follow the command that He issued to Peter. Stop calling unclean what He has declared holy.

PRAYER OF DECLARATION:

Father, forgive me for ever calling unclean that which You have declared clean. Thank You for the complete cleansing I experienced through the blood of Jesus. By Your grace, help me renew my mind and realign my thinking to this reality. I am holy, chosen, purified, cleansed and set apart for Your service and delight.

Your Wildly Generous Prince

For God has proved his love by giving us his greatest treasure, the gift of his Son. And since God freely offered him up as the sacrifice for us all, he certainly won't withhold from us anything else he has to give.

ROMANS 8:32

Imagine for a moment that a rich and powerful prince falls wildly in love with a poor peasant girl and chooses her to be his bride. As a token of his love and devotion in advance of their wedding, he bestows upon her an engagement gift of extraordinary value and price.

Now imagine that, a few days later, she approaches her royal fiancé with a small but urgent need. Her cottage cupboard is out of bread. She asks if she might receive a loaf from his vast and ever-busy palace bakery. But her fiancé's response is, "No. I love you, but you cannot have a loaf of bread."

If you were to hear of such a thing, you would question either the prince's love or his sanity. And rightly so. After giving the object of his affection a gift of incalculable worth, it would make no sense to withhold from his beloved something as simple as a needed loaf of bread.

This is precisely Paul's point in today's key verse. To win our hearts and bring us into intimate relationship with Himself, God has already bestowed the most lavish and extravagant gift imaginable—His own precious Son. With Him came (past tense) everything pertaining to life and godliness we could possibly need. (2 Peter 1:3)

Yet, so often we approach our heavenly Father as if He is not wildly generous and unspeakably good. Or as if His resources are scarce. Our God is neither miserly nor poor. And He cares very much about even our smallest needs.

It is no accident our sweet Savior's first public miracle was the simple provision of some wine on a rural couple's wedding day. This was no life-or-death crisis. The parents would have survived the embarrassment before their friends and family. But the mere prospect of their public humiliation was cause enough to draw forth wonder-working power from the Son of God.

Here is the glorious, comforting, liberating truth: God has given you His first and best. Everything else you need is small change. So, please do not insult His extravagant love by coming to Him like a beggar—or as if you need to find some way to overcome His reluctance to supply your needs and bless you. He is generous. He loves you. And your heavenly Father proved His love by giving you His greatest treasure, the gift of his Son. He certainly won't withhold from You anything else He has to give.

PRAYER OF DECLARATION:

Wonderful Father, forgive me for any time I have approached You as if You were anything less than extravagantly generous. Or if my heart has ever seemed to question Your goodness. Your gift of Jesus shouts of Your love and compassion toward me. I come to You with confidence and expectancy, as one who knows she's adored.

The Incredible Power
You Possess

Sharing words of wisdom is satisfying to your inner being.
It encourages you to know that you've changed someone else's life.
Your words are so powerful that they will kill or give life…

PROVERBS 18:20—21

Jesus talked to trees. Well, He did on at least one occasion. In passing a barren fig tree one day, using it as a prophetic metaphor for the nation, Jesus spoke these words to the fruitless plant: "No one will ever eat fruit from you again!" When the disciples walked by that tree the next day, it had completely withered and died.

On another occasion, Jesus spoke to a little boy's sack lunch— just a chunk of bread and a few small fish. In this case, Jesus spoke words over the food that caused it to multiply and feed thousands, with bushels left over.

Clearly, Jesus' words carried great power. But according to the Bible, yours do as well. That's the message of today's key scripture and dozens of others in God's Word. In speaking to trees and fish sandwiches, Jesus was doing something the Bible calls cursing and blessing.

This did not just apply to Jesus. Your words are more powerful than you know. This power flows from the spiritual reality that we are God's image-bearers in the Earth…royal priests who carry Jesus' authority…containers of His grace ready to spill out supernatural power to anyone in need. This gives our words enormous weight in both the natural and spiritual worlds. Angels attend to our declarations. Things in the heavenlies move and change in response to our proclamations. And one of the most powerful uses of our words is the God-given power to bless.

The Greek word frequently translated "bless" in the New Testament is *eulogeo*. It means "to speak well of someone or something." In fact, it's the source for our common word eulogy, a speech in which a person is praised and honored.

Blessing has an opposite: cursing. Both carry spiritual power. Both are spoken. James once marveled at believers who use the same mouth to utter both blessings and curses. (James 3:10)

Every believer possesses the vastly underappreciated power to bless. In his wonderful book, *The Power to Bless*, my friend Alan Wright writes, "I'm convinced that, other than God's work through prayer, blessing is the most powerful tool for change in the world. It's not magic. It's thoroughly biblical."[2] It's true. By the indwelling Spirit of God, you are abundantly equipped to create blessing by speaking blessing everywhere you go.

PRAYER OF DECLARATION:

Oh, Father, what power You have entrusted to me—the power to bless. May I be a messenger of Your grace as I speak life to those around me. I happily yield my mouth to Your Spirit today, heavenly Father, to speak blessing and words of refreshment to the weary and hope to the discouraged.

Holy Audacity

And now we are brothers and sisters in God's family because of the blood of Jesus, and he welcomes us to come into the most holy sanctuary in the heavenly realm—boldly and without hesitation. For he has dedicated a new life-giving way for us to approach God. For just as the veil was torn in two, Jesus' body was torn open to give us free and fresh access to him! And since we now have a magnificent High Priest to welcome us into God's house, we come closer to God and approach him with an open heart, fully convinced that nothing will keep us at a distance from him. For our hearts have been sprinkled with blood to remove impurity, and we have been freed from an accusing conscience. Now we are clean, unstained, and presentable to God inside and out!

HEBREWS 10:19–22

"I've sinned." "I haven't had a quiet time in weeks." "I screamed at my kids." "I'm a terrible, selfish person who thinks terrible thoughts."

For most believers, every approach to God's throne to ask for help or favor is accompanied by a whirlwind of disqualifying thoughts. Sound familiar? That's a big problem because confident expectancy before God is a major key to receiving from Him in prayer.

In the face of this routine storm of self-accusation and self-condemnation, many believers give up on even making a request of God. They tell themselves they need to get their act together and become a little more "deserving" first—then they'll come to God for help.

Those who do manage to make it to God's throne slink in sheepishly, laden with guilt and a crushing sense of unworthiness. When their prayers prove to be ineffective, they're not all that surprised. Faith moves mountains. And people who have disqualified themselves have no faith. There's a better way.

Remember the desperate, hemorrhaging woman who pressed through the crowd to merely put one finger on the edge of Jesus' tunic? And this, in flagrant violation of Jewish social regulations. Such boldness. What glorious nerve! This was an audacity born of supreme confidence in two things: Jesus' power and His goodness.

That bold woman had access to divine power and goodness because it (He) was walking through the center of her village. As today's rich, key passage reveals, you have far easier access to Him because of what Jesus accomplished for you through His death and resurrection.

It's vital to continually refresh your awareness of Christ's finished work on the cross. Why? Because, through that purifying work, you qualify. You qualify! In Christ, you qualify for access, connection, favor, blessing, and help in time of need. So, come with holy audacity!

Prayer of Declaration:

Father, I thank You that my access to Your power and goodness is not linked to my personal qualifications or my good behavior. I come boldly to You today because Jesus' sinless body was torn to open the way for me. I know if I can get to You, good things flow to me. And getting to You is easy because I'm coming in and through Jesus. My hopes are up and my expectations, high.

The Offense of Asking Small

Never doubt God's mighty power to work in you and accomplish all this.
He will achieve infinitely more than your greatest request,
your most unbelievable dream, and exceed your wildest imagination!
He will outdo them all, for his miraculous power constantly energizes you.

Ephesians 3:20

The young fundraiser for a local charitable organization fidgeted nervously in the leather chair seated across from a mahogany desk so big it looked like you could land an airplane on it. She was making her first big solo call on a major donor prospect— the silver-haired Christian owner of a prominent local business. She had presented a meticulously prepared folder of information and walked the gentlemen through each page and graph, detailing all the good work the charity was doing and highlighting some key future projects that would need funding.

On the final page she revealed the amount of the donation she had decided to ask for—a five-figure sum that felt enormous to her. He had been studying that page silently for a minute or two. The longer he stared at it, the more uncomfortable she grew. *Had she asked for too much?*

Finally, he broke the silence. "I'm willing to help your organization. But you need to go back and do some homework. Then come back and see me." She did and discovered she had not asked for too much but rather too little. This wealthy man routinely made six-figure donations to the causes he chose to support. He was mildly offended by what he viewed as a small request.

How often do we do something similar with our generous heavenly Father? Believers who have not renewed their minds to the realities of God's abundant grace and goodness come to Him with low expectations and small requests. This is often because our conception of God's character and disposition has been warped by religion. The actual terms of the New Covenant sound too good to be true—so we assume they are.

This, in turn, produces a puny prayer life that doesn't ever seem to move very much of heaven to Earth. Not surprisingly, coming to God half-convinced you don't really qualify for help, answers, or favor is not a prescription for moving mountains.

The fact is, God wants us to ask big. Indeed, He *needs* us to ask boldly and ambitiously because He wants to do big things in the Earth through us. He has chosen to partner with us in extending His Kingdom and seeing His will done on Earth.

For this very reason Jesus gave us what is, in essence, a blank check: "For I will do whatever you ask me to do when you ask me in my name. And that is how the Son will show what the Father is really like and bring glory to him. Ask me anything in my name, and I will do it for you!" (John 14:13–14)

PRAYER OF DECLARATION:

Father, I will not doubt Your mighty power to work in me, through me, and for me. Nor will I insult Your grace by approaching You as if You are not utterly good and generous. I come ready to partner with You in seeing Your will done on Earth just as it is in heaven. By Your Spirit, inform and guide my asking!

The Words That Unleash Heaven's Power

Let everyone thank God, for he is good, and he is easy to please!
His tender love for us continues on forever!

PSALM 136:1

There is no such thing as "magic words." But if the Bible contains something akin to them, it is the two sentences that make up today's key verse. This phrase, with only slight variations, is repeated numerous times in the Scriptures. Some other translations render this: "Give thanks to the Lord, for he is good! His faithful love endures forever." (NLT)

In 1 Chronicles 16, we see the first recorded appearance of these extraordinary words in a song penned by King David to celebrate the bringing of the Ark of Covenant (and therefore the presence of God) back to the center of Israelite life. At the climax of a long, exuberant hymn of praise, David, the extraordinary lyricist, sings them. (v.36 NLT)

The Bible reports that, on several other occasions, the unified saying or singing of these words by a group of people was accompanied by either a miraculous deliverance or a tangible manifestation of God's presence and power—or both. For example, in 2 Chronicles chapter five, the singing of these special words resulted in the very glory of God Himself filling the room in a cloud-like fashion—becoming so intense that no one present could even stay on their feet.

In the 20th chapter of that same book, we see the Israelites going out into battle to face an overwhelmingly superior enemy. The army is led by the worshipers singing David's powerful lyrics. Suddenly, the enemy armies become confused and turn on each other. The attackers are destroyed without a single Israelite sword being unsheathed.

These words repeatedly appear in the Psalms of David and in one of Jeremiah's prophecies. These may very well be the most frequently repeated phrases in all of the Bible. Why are they so obviously important and so clearly powerful? Why do these phrases seem to unleash heaven's power on earth?

It's not the words themselves. It's God's people giving voice, in faith and adoration, to the truth they contain that releases power and glory. This declaration is a mighty cord woven of three strands: (1) a heart of gratitude; (2) an affirmation of God's goodness; and (3) a reminder that God's love is covenantal and, therefore, relentless.

When you contemplate the truth that an utterly good God's love is tenacious and impervious to your frailty, flaws, and wavering faithfulness, the heart has only one rational response: To cry, "Thank You!" And when we utter that cry together, it rends the very fabric separating heaven from earth, allowing glory and power to pour down.

Prayer of Declaration

When I recognize that You are utterly and completely good and that You have fastened Your great love upon me with the unbreakable cords of covenant, the only rational response is gratitude.

So, Father, this is my heart's cry to You: I give You thanks because You are utterly good, and Your faithful, tenacious love for me never ends!

The King has a Message for You

When I saw him, I fell down at his feet as good as dead, but he laid his right hand on me and I heard his reassuring voice saying: Don't yield to fear. I am the Beginning and I am the End, the Living One! I was dead, but now look—I am alive forever and ever. And I hold the keys that unlock death and the unseen world.

REVELATION 1:17—18

The Apostle John knew Jesus better than any person who ever lived. He was part of the Savior's inner circle of three. And even among those three, John held a special place. They were friends. One day, while in exile on the island of Patmos, decades after Jesus' resurrection and ascension, John is caught up into heaven for a surprise visit with His friend and Savior.

Yes, John knew Jesus but had never seen Him the crowned, ruling King. It was, to say the least, a startling sight. Jesus' voice is like thunder; His hair white; His eyes flaming like fire; His feet glowing like molten brass, and His face shining like the sun.

John is so overwhelmed at a mere glimpse of this King that he collapses in a heap like a dead man. Suddenly, among the quaking, John feels the warmth of a hand on his shoulder. He knows that hand. Then he hears the voice of his old friend. In today's key passage, John recorded the words he heard. In it, Jesus packs a lifetime's worth of comfort and reassurance into four simple sentences. Let's examine Jesus' message, piece-by-piece:

- "Don't yield to fear." There is no place for fear in the presence of such love and power.

- "I am the Beginning and I am the End." In the Greek, "the Alpha and Omega," the A-to-Z. He is the author and the finisher. All of creation began with Him and now is being remade through Him.

- I am "the Living One." King Jesus is not only alive, but He is also Life itself. He is the Tree of Life from the Garden of Eden. Connection to Him imparts wholeness and immortality.

- "I was dead." He had to die. He had to taste death in order to defeat it. He had to die *our* death so we could partake of His life.

- "But now look, I am alive forever and ever." And yet here He stands before us, gloriously alive, and will be so forever. And because He will live forever, those of us who have partaken of His life will live eternally as well.

- "And I hold the keys that unlock death and the unseen world." Only the One who holds the keys can release the prisoners.

The words Jesus spoke to John weren't only for him. They are for you. Today. Don't yield to fear, for He is both the beginning and the end. He died for you, yet He is "the Living One" who gives you everlasting life because He holds the keys of Death. He is your King. And today, you can feel that reassuring hand on your shoulder, too. Because He is your friend.

Prayer of Declaration

Jesus, my King, how great You are! Of course, I will not yield to fear. Your love and power keep me safely in Your hand. You were dead, but You conquered Death, not just for Yourself but for me, as well. You are the "Living One." You don't just give me life; You *are* Life. You hold the keys—to eternity and to my heart. I feel Your strong, gentle hand of comfort on my shoulder. I hear Your reassuring voice.

About the Author

David A. Holland is a writer, speaker, teacher, husband, father, and grandfather—carrying a call to help God's people better comprehend His extraordinary goodness and extravagant grace.

He is the founding pastor-teacher of The Cup & Table Co., a network of house churches based in the Dallas-Fort Worth area wherein New Covenant truths are proclaimed, and the implications of Jesus' finished work are celebrated and lived out. His writing on faith, life, and culture is accessible at DavidAHolland.com.

Twitter: @DavidHolland

Instagram: DavidAHolland

Facebook: @DavidAHolland.Inspiration

Endnotes

1   Jean Kim, "Why are Women So Exhausted, *Psychology Today, (September 26, 2017), https://www.psychologytoday.com/us/blog/culture-shrink/201709/why-are-women-so-exhausted*

2   Alan Wright, *The Power to Bless,* Baker Books, Grand Rapids, (2021), p. 23